CHARACTERISTICS OF USERS OF REFUND ANTICIPATION LOANS AND REFUND ANTICIPATION CHECKS

Prepared for the US Department of the Treasury by the Urban Institute, 2010

Authors of this report are:

Brett Theodos, Urban Institute

Rachel Brash, Urban Institute

Jessica F. Compton, Urban Institute

Karen Masken, IRS

Nancy Pindus, Urban Institute

C. Eugene Steuerle, Urban Institute

Acknowledgments

This report was completed under contract to the U.S. Department of the Treasury under Order Number GS23F8198H/T09BPA017, with funds authorized by the U.S. Department of the Treasury.

Oversight and review were provided by the Treasury Department's Office of Financial Education and Financial Access. The report benefited from the experience, advice, and review of Doug Wissoker, Signe-Mary McKernan, and Caroline Ratcliffe. We owe a special thanks to the IRS Office of Research, Analysis, and Statistics, for making available their data and analytical expertise.

The Urban Institute is a nonprofit, nonpartisan policy research and educational organization that examines the social, economic, and governance problems facing the nation. The views expressed are those of the authors and should not be attributed to the Urban Institute, its trustees, or its funders.

Table of Contents

INTRODUCTION — 1

BACKGROUND ON RALS/RACS AND THE CHANGING INDUSTRY LANDSCAPE — 3
- What RALs/RACs Are and How They Work — 3
- RAL and RAC Use Over Time — 5
- Major Industry Players — 6
- Changes in the Industry — 7

WHO USES RALS AND RACS — 8
- Review of the Literature — 8
- Data and Methods — 9
- Descriptive Analyses — 10
- The Correlates of RAL/RAC Use — 21

WHY TAXPAYERS USE RALS/RACS AND WHY TAX PREPARERS OFFER THEM — 28
- Data and Methods — 28
- Borrower Motivations — 28
- Supplier Motivations — 31

CONCLUSION — 33

REFERENCES — 34

METHODS AND DATA APPENDIX — 37
- IRS Administrative and Secondary Data — 39
- Insights From Stakeholders — 41

SUPPLEMENTAL APPENDIX — 43

INTRODUCTION

Refund anticipation loans (RALs) are bank loans secured by the taxpayer's expected refund and Refund anticipation checks (RACs) are temporary bank accounts established on behalf of a taxpayer into which a direct deposit refund can be received. The goal of this project is to provide greater information on the characteristics of RAL/RAC users and why they choose these products.

We find that among the most important characteristics influencing RAL/RAC use were lower income, young adulthood, single head-of-household filing status, receipt of the Earned Income Tax Credit (EITC), and use of a paid preparer. We also find that RALs and RACs are highly spatially concentrated and that living in the poorest communities is associated with dramatic increases in use of these products, even after controlling for a taxpayer's income and filing status. Also, for the first time, we found some unique differences in the use of RALs versus RACs according to such variables as military status. Finally, we find that individuals with any interest and dividend income used RALs and RACs to a much smaller degree than did those with otherwise similar characteristics.

RALs and RACs are used by one in seven tax filers—and more than one in six filers who receive refunds. Taxpayers are able to receive their refunds more quickly than a mailed check by using RALs, often in one to three days. RACs are no quicker than other IRS direct deposit returns, but for those who lack a bank account, and/or would receive a paper check, they may speed up receipt of refund by up to six weeks. Both RALs and RACs enable payment of tax preparation fees out of the expected refund.

To gain a better understanding of RAL/RACs, this report is broadly divided into two sets of research questions. The first examines who obtains them and who does not and what demographic, economic, and geographic factors are associated with the use of these products. Using individual-level IRS tax-filing data from tax year 2008, we provide descriptive breakdowns of many individual and geographical characteristics that are linked with use of RALs/RACs. We then run cross-sectional taxpayer-level multivariate models to explain what characteristics are associated with take-up of RALs/RACs, including both personal factors that are captured in individual level tax administration data as well as local factors compiled from several (non-IRS) administrative data sets. This quantitative analysis was conducted on IRS-provided data on millions of tax filers who received a refund in tax year 2008. With this data set, findings are statistically significant for the population of US tax filers.

The second set of research questions examines why these products exist, using interviews with industry stakeholders. This research was qualitative in nature. What motivates taxpayers to use RALs and RACs? What role do tax preparers play? And what other (and lower-cost) credit options are available at tax time for low-income taxpayers? To address these questions, we conducted 18 interviews with 11 organizations: tax preparers, RAL/RAC providers, RAL/RAC tax form software developers, low-cost RAL lenders, and Volunteer Income Tax Assistance (VITA) program sites that provide free tax preparation services and partner with low-cost RAL lenders. We found, in summary, that most RAL and RAC recipients use these products to pay for pressing financial obligations, both expected and unexpected, and for their tax preparation. RAL/RAC users, particularly those claiming the EITC, are driven to paid preparers by the complexity of filing a tax return. Stakeholders from the RAL/RAC industry do not feel that consumers use these products because they fail to understand that they are loans or because they are not aware of the fees involved. Consumer advocates disagree, claiming that use is partly driven by aggressive, targeted marketing.

In appendices, we provide a detailed discussion of the quantitative and qualitative data and analytical methods, and supplementary tables and maps.

Background on RALs/RACs and the Changing Industry Landscape

What RALs/RACs Are and How They Work

Refund anticipation loans (RALs) are interest-bearing loans made by banks, facilitated by tax preparers and tax preparer software, that allow taxpayers to receive an advance on their tax refund from the IRS. A RAL's amount is based on the taxpayer's anticipated income tax refund (minus tax preparation fees and additional loan and preparation fees) and secured by and directly repaid from the taxpayer's IRS refund. With refund anticipation checks (RACs), the bank opens a temporary bank account into which the IRS directly deposits the refund check. The bank waits until the IRS directly deposits the consumer's refund into the account and then issues the consumer a paper check or debit card, minus fees for tax preparation and the cost of the product. Consumers who already have bank accounts also can receive their refunds using direct deposit, but without any fees attached. Unlike RAL users, RAC users do not receive their money earlier than other filers using direct deposit.

Timing. It is often believed that individuals are able to receive their refunds more quickly by using RALs and RACs. When using a RAL, clients receive the loan the same day or one to two days later (there is often an extra charge for receiving the RAL the same day). However, with a RAC, money is only deposited into the client's temporary bank account after the IRS processes and directly deposits the refund. Therefore, at least historically, clients wait 9 to 15 days before receiving the refund, minus fees (Internal Revenue Service 2009). These products do not typically produce faster payment than waiting for a return from the IRS that is directly deposited into a taxpayer's bank account. However, taxpayers who do not have a bank account (or do not wish to directly deposit their returns) can wait up to eight weeks to receive their refunds by mail.

Revenues and pricing.[1]

While modest in amount, concentrated in poor communities, and generally used in the first few weeks of the tax season, RALs and RACs are not a small industry. Over 18 percent of tax filers with refunds receive one of these products. By one estimate, consumers paid approximately $833 million in RAL fees in 2006 and $740 million in 2007 (Wu and Fox 2010). The size of this market results in significant income. For example, in 2009 H&R Block brought in $142.7 million in revenue through RALs, plus an additional $22.7 million in revenues from the Emerald Advance card, representing about 5.5 percent of

---

[1] In recent years, the loan funds were made available to the taxpayer only after the IRS had indicated that the taxpayer had no outstanding debts—such as child support or student loan payments—that might offset the taxpayer's refund. In August 2010, the IRS announced that the mechanism by which it alerts tax preparers and RAL lenders of these outstanding debts, referred to as the debt indicator, would no longer be available beginning in the 2011 tax season. For more information, see the following section of this report, The Changing RAL/RAC Landscape.

tax services revenue. In 2008, Jackson Hewitt derived 24 percent of its revenues from financial products.[2]

RAL and RAC recipients generally pay for their tax preparation with their refund anticipation loans or checks. Tax preparation fees vary by provider. At H&R Block, they average $187, and have been found to be as high as $350 (Wu and Fox 2010). In addition to tax preparation costs, RAL and RAC consumers pay fees to access these financial products. It is difficult to calculate the average cost of a RAL or RAC as pricing varies considerably across and within providers, and much of the industry does not publicly report on the fees that are paid by consumers. Further complicating matters is the fact that the industry has generally "unbundled" its fees, making pricing comparisons more difficult. Still, most tax preparers charge a flat fee for setting up a RAL or RAC account, the price of which typically ranges from $30 to $35. RAL recipients pay an additional fee that is a fraction of the loan amount, usually around 1 percent. Providers charge additional fees of $25 to $55 if customers want to receive their RAL on the same day as they apply for a refund. Other fees for document preparation, applying, processing, e-filing, transmission, and technology often also apply. For example, H&R Block charges $20 to receive a paper check, a fee that was paid by one in three H&R Block RAL recipients (Wu and Fox 2010). Before it left the market in April 2010, JPMorgan Chase charged an additional $10 "technology access fee." Jackson Hewitt will allow franchisees to charge up to $40 for "data and document storage." Some of these fees are set by tax software firms, while others are established by the lender or tax preparer. Independent RAL and RAC providers, which make up roughly 40 percent of the RAL market, often charge additional fees as well (Wu and Fox 2010). If after applying, a taxpayer is rejected from receiving a RAL, then he or she is usually automatically given a RAC, with its fees. All fees are deducted from the final RAL/RAC amount issued to the taxpayer once he or she is approved. If the RAL or RAC customer does not receive the expected tax return amount as calculated by the tax preparer, he or she is liable to the lender for the difference between the expected amount and the actual amount, additional interest, and other fees, as applicable.

Regulation. RALs are principally regulated by the federal government. The Truth in Lending Act, enacted in 1968, requires all lenders to state the interest rates for all loans as annual percentage rates (APR). The average term on RALs is one to two weeks, the length of time it takes for the bank to receive payment on the loan in the form of the refund from the IRS. The federal government prohibits tax preparers from making the loans directly and therefore requires an intermediary (there may be two intermediaries if the tax preparer does not have custom loan transmission software). Federal rules also regulate disclosure of these products to taxpayers. For example, a tax preparer arranging a RAL or RAC must secure the taxpayer's written consent to provide tax information to the lender.

---

[2] From Wu and Fox (2010), whose data sources are annual financial statements filed by H&R Block and Jackson Hewitt with the Securities and Exchange Commission.

RAL and RAC Use Over Time

The refund anticipation loan was created in the 1980s as a short-term loan secured by a taxpayer's tax refund. Beneficial Finance came up with the concept of a short-term tax-time loan, and H&R Block partnered with the consumer finance company to offer these "instant tax refunds" (Rivlin 2010). Other banks to become major players in the market over the following decade and a half were Bank One, JPMorgan Chase, HSBC, Republic Bank & Trust Company, and Santa Barbara Bank & Trust. The RAL quickly became popular among recipients of the EITC. EITC recipients and others saw the loans as an attractive way to receive their tax refunds, which could be substantial, in a few days rather than weeks, and to pay for tax preparation out of the refund. The refund anticipation check was introduced as a lower-cost alternative that was not a loan, but created a temporary account into which the taxpayer's refund was deposited and deferred payment of the tax preparation and RAC fees until receipt of the refund.

As RAL use grew through the 1990s and tax preparation firms expanded their outlets across the United States, consumers and providers responded to several policy changes. In the early 1990s, the IRS provided the industry a "direct deposit indicator," a screening tool to alert RAL lenders of debts collectible by the federal government that might offset a taxpayer's refund, including tax debt, child support, and student debts. This was an important risk mitigation tool for lenders, who faced difficulty collecting payment on the refund loan should the refund arrive at an amount less than the loan provided to the borrower. In late 1994, the IRS stopped offering the indicator because of concerns about fraud in electronically filed returns with RALs. Subsequently, the number of RALs fell from 9.5 million in 1994 to 6 million in 1999. Fees also increased once the non-indicator policy was implemented. In 2000, the IRS reinstated the screening tool, which it then termed the "debt indicator." The use of RALs grew substantially, more than doubling in two years to a peak of 12.7 million in 2002 (figure 1). The IRS saw the debt indicator as a means of encouraging electronic filing and direct deposit. In the last several years, the use of RALs has decreased as they were eclipsed by the use of the relatively lower-cost RACs. By 2009, RAL use had declined to 6.9 million users, while RAC use grew to 12.9 million users.

FIGURE 1: NUMBER OF RALS AND RACS (IN MILLIONS), 2000-2009

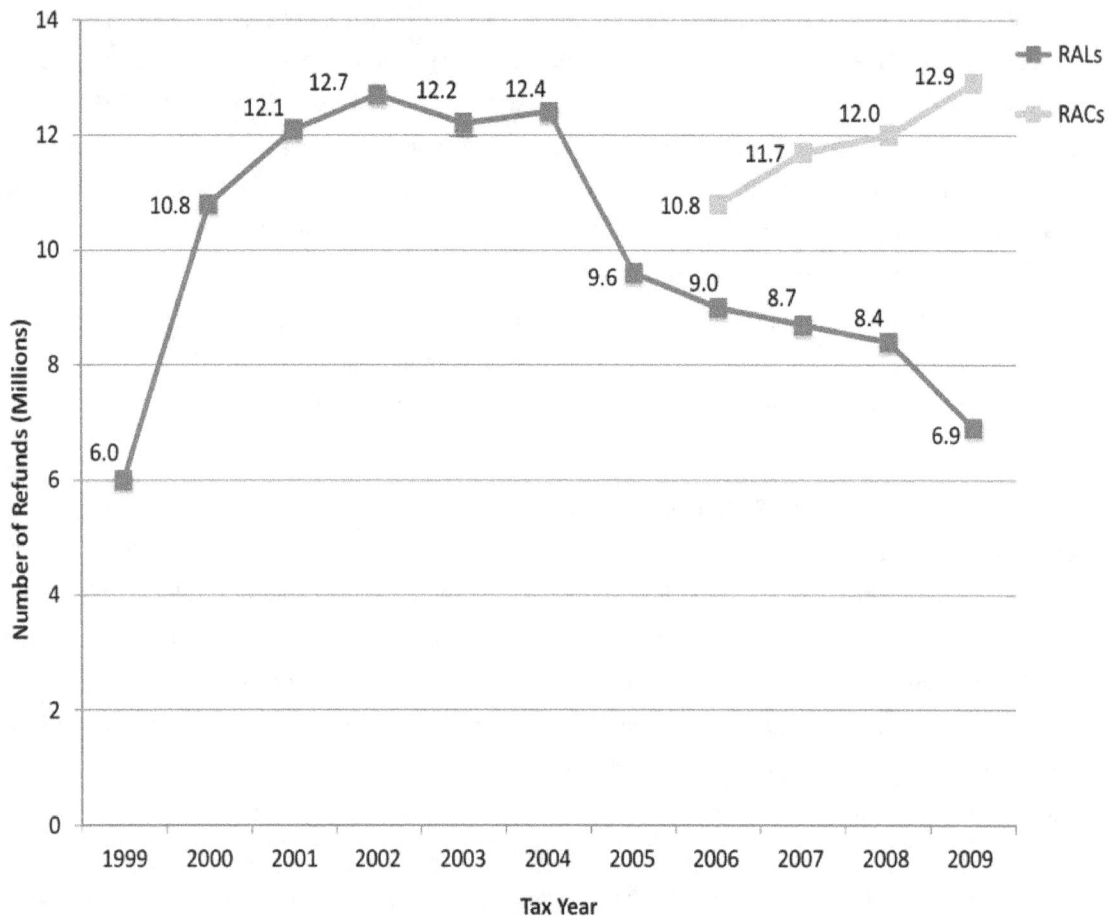

Sources: Wu 2005, GAO 2009, Wu and Fox 2010, and authors' analysis of IRS data.

Major Industry Players

The major players involved in the industry are: RAL/RAC lenders, tax preparation firms, and transmitters, or software makers, whose software is necessary for electronically filing tax returns and issuing bank products (table 2). Playing a minor role within the market are low-cost RAL providers, often in partnership with VITA sites. There were six major RAL and RAC lenders as of September 2010.

Four major tax preparation firms are H&R Block, Jackson Hewitt, Liberty Tax Service, and Instant Tax Service. Independent preparers have about 40 percent of the RAL market. H&R Block is the country's largest tax preparation chain, preparing about 16.5 million individual tax returns in 2008, about 3.85 million of

Table 2: Major Players in the RAL/RAC Industry

Tax Preparers	H&R Block, Jackson Hewitt, Liberty Tax Service, Instant Tax Service
Lenders	HSBC, Refund Advantage (Louisville, KY), Republic Bank & Trust (Louisville, KY), River City Bank (Louisville, KY), Santa Barbara Tax Products Group, MetaBank (Storm Lake, IA)
Transmitters	CCH Small Firm Services, Drake Software, Intuit, TaxSlayer
Recently Departed Industry Players	JPMorgan Chase, Santa Barbara Bank & Trust

Note: HSBC has stopped funding all RALs except those offered through its contract with H&R Block.

which had RALs associated with them (Wu and Fox 2010). Jackson Hewitt prepared about 3.4 million returns in 2008, about 1.2 million of which had RALs associated with them. The proportion of its customers receiving RALs was higher than H&R Block's, about 35 percent compared to 23 percent. Jackson Hewitt's founder, John Hewitt, left the firm in 1996 (Liberty Tax Service 2010) and started what is now the third-largest tax preparation chain with about 3,200 locations, Liberty Tax Service. The use of RALs and RACs is even higher at this firm—in 2008, about 37 percent of Liberty's customers received a RAL and another 37 percent received a RAC.

RALs and RACs could not be provided without computer software to process the tax returns and bank products. The largest tax preparation chains have created their own custom transmitting software, but independent tax preparers rely on software companies, or transmitters, to set up tax-time loan accounts. These products include TaxWise and ATX from CCH Small Firm Services. Individual users of Intuit's TurboTax can receive a RAC using the software, but not a RAL. Unlike RACs issued through tax preparation firms, which come in the form of a check or debit card and do not require a bank account, RACs issued online cannot be issued in check form and require an existing account. That account can either be a traditional bank account or a pre-paid card, which in some cases customers can purchase at the same time they are purchasing their RAC.

A number of free and low-cost RAL providers exist around the country, the oldest of which is Alternatives Federal Credit Union. These programs provide free tax preparation or are linked to VITA sites that provide free tax preparation. The programs emerged largely as a way to entice taxpayers away from higher-cost RALs. They do not provide a large number of RALs—from fewer than a hundred to a few thousand.

Changes in the Industry

The industry has recently lost several large players who became increasingly concerned about the growing stigma attached to RALs and RACs. JPMorgan Chase, the RAL lender for about 13,000 independent preparers, left the market in late April 2010 (the end of tax year 2009), concerned that the risk to its reputation from providing these high-cost loans outweighed their profitability (Eichenbaum and Donmoyer 2010). Similarly, the only other large international bank involved in RALs, HSBC, the lender for H&R Block, may be poised to leave the RAL market because of the IRS's decision to withhold the debt indicator. In response to HSBC missing a deadline to submit proposed fees, credit criteria, and qualifying procedures for the 2011 tax season, H&R Block filed suit in mid October 2010, alleging breach of contract (Nish 2010). HSBC had recently stopped issuing these loans to independent preparers and had already indicated that it might exit the market altogether when its contract with H&R Block expired in 2013. Prior to the 2009 tax season, Santa Barbara Bank & Trust (SBBT), a subsidiary of Pacific Capital Bancorp, also left the market. Pacific's regulator, the OCC, withheld approval for the bank to make RALs given their level of troubled assets. (SBBT was able to sell its RAL/RAC business to form Santa Barbara Tax Products Group, which is expected to provide RALs and RACs in the 2010 tax season.)

Who Uses RALs and RACs

Of 111 million tax filers with a refund in tax year 2008, 8.4 million (7.6 percent) took out a RAL and another 11.6 million (10.5 percent) received a RAC. By examining who uses RALs and RACs, we can better understand the demand for these products. While several studies have looked at who uses these products, this research advances the knowledge base in several ways. A joint effort by researchers at the Urban Institute and the IRS Office of Research, Analysis, and Statistics allowed quantitative estimates to be made on the basis of a large number of actual tax records, while completely protecting taxpayers' confidentiality. This approach provides several advantages over alternatives. First, we analyze millions of taxpayer records. Second, for determining actual use, administrative data are more reliable than survey data, which rely on less accurate recall. Third, many other studies had to rely upon publically available aggregate zip code–level variables. Taxpayer-level data allow the use of multivariate techniques to isolate the effects of various demographic, economic, and geographic characteristics on the take-up of advance refund products. Fourth, tax records provide reliable data on such items as age, adjusted gross income (AGI), filing status, gender for single and head-of-household filers, and geographical location. Fifth, these data also allow us to make distinctions between RAL and RAC use not always possible for other researchers. And finally, the influence of characteristics associated with place has been underexplored in previous research. We were able to provide a much finer breakdown on the prevalence of RAL/RAC use by state and even zip code, with wide variation across the country, within states, and between more urban and rural areas. On the other hand, the IRS does not collect information on other household characteristics, for example, education levels, occupations, race/ethnicity, and nativity, so our analysis cannot explore their relationship to patterns of RAL and RAC use.

Review of the Literature

The characteristics of RAL/RAC users tend to be similar to consumers of other alternative financial services (AFS) products. Most AFS product users are young adults from low-income households (FINRA Investor Education Foundation 2009; Feltner 2007). Patterns and frequency of use are also similar among AFS consumers. Unlike other AFS products such as pawnshop loans or payday loans, RALs and RACs can only be provided once in the year—at tax refund time. As a result, repeated use can only be tracked over a number of years. There is some evidence to suggest that RAL and RAC consumers are frequently repeat users and purchase the product out of habit (Barr and Dokko 2008; Elliehausen 2005).

The largest group of RAL/RAC consumers is recipients of the EITC. The EITC is the largest means-tested anti-poverty program in the United States, a $49 billion income transfer to the nation's working poor. Wu and Fox (2010) estimate that EITC recipients who took out RALs spent $1.5 billion accessing their refunds ($507 million in RAL loan and additional fees plus $991 million in tax preparation fees). This measure of EITC program funds consumed would be significantly higher if RAC fees and check cashing fees were also included.

A second important and partially overlapping group that uses RALs/RACs is the unbanked—those who have no bank account. There are many reasons people are unbanked, including personal credit problems, inconvenient bank hours or locations, minimum account balance requirements, uncomfortable or unwelcoming environments at financial institutions, and high fees for bounced checks or low account balances (Federal Deposit Insurance Corporation 2009). According to a recent national survey of 1,488 U.S. households, unbanked households are twice as likely to get tax advances (FINRA Investor Education Foundation 2009). Our work in this project finds a very large difference in RAL/RAC use among those with and without interest and dividend income. (We take the presence of interest and dividend income to be a proxy for banking status, although some of the banked could have only non-interest bearing accounts.)

RAL/RAC users are disproportionately younger, low income, and from impoverished communities. RAL/RAC users are more likely to have children and are more likely to be single heads of households (Elliehausen 2005; Masken et al. 2008). RAL users have less formal education than those who do not get an advance refund. An analysis of national survey data found that 11.2 percent of those without a high school degree received a RAL in the past five years, compared with just 2.7 percent of those who graduated college (McKernan, Ratcliffe, and Kuehn 2010). These characteristics suggest that many of these individuals are more susceptible to income shocks.

Researchers have found that use of RALs and RACs is higher among ethnic minorities and communities of color. In data from a national survey of self-reported RAL use, FINRA Investor Education Foundation (2009) found that whereas 13 percent of African Americans and 9 percent of Hispanics reported using a RAL in the last five years, just 6 percent of whites did. Using 2006 tax data, Duda, Buitrago, and Smith (2010) found that in Illinois, RAL usage is higher in African American communities, controlling for EITC status. Keeley, Ludwig, and Griffith (2007) also found that RALs were highly concentrated in minority neighborhoods in New York City. In an analysis of Native American lands, Dewees and Parish (2009) found ethnicity to be a predictor of RAL use, controlling for other factors. In 9 of the 10 states examined, Native communities had higher rates of RAL use among EITC recipients than other counties in the state. They suggest that patterns of RAL use in some Native communities may be different than other rural areas.

Several studies demonstrate that taxpayer purchases of RALs differ widely across the country and vary by urbanization. Analyses of both administrative and survey data find that RAL/RAC users are more likely to live in the South compared to other regions of the United States (Federal Deposit Insurance Corporation 2009; Masken et al. 2008). Berube and Kornblatt (2005) find that similar variation exists within metropolitan areas and cities. Dewees and Parish (2009) find that a greater level of urbanization is a predictor of higher rates of RAL use. However, as noted earlier, many of the counties with the highest use of RALs among EITC filers using a paid preparer are in very remote rural counties with reservations (Dewees and Parish 2009).

Data and Methods

We analyze IRS data from tax years 2005 through 2008. Using these data, we first run descriptive analyses on the universe of tax filers 18 years or older with refunds (111 million filers in TY 2008). We only examine returns with refunds, as those owing money make no use of RALs or RACs. It is important to note that tax filers do not always equate to households or families as they are conventionally defined, as families could be composed of multiple tax filers. For this research, the IRS shared only aggregate statistics with Urban Institute researchers.

To isolate the influence of individual factors on the decision to take up a RAL or RAC, we estimate multinomial logistic regressions. For these multivariate analyses, we create a 1 percent sample of U.S. taxpayers in TY 2005 and TY 2008. For explanatory variables, we include taxpayer-level characteristics: the refund amount and how it was prepared (self-prepared, paid preparer, or volunteer preparer), filing status/gender, receipt of the EITC (with and without qualifying children), number of dependent children living at home, age, adjusted gross income (AGI), interest and dividend income, unemployment compensation, and military status.

In addition to taxpayers' demographic, economic, and tax return characteristics, we incorporate secondary data about the communities where taxpayers live. We assemble geographic information from the Federal Deposit Insurance Corporation (FDIC), the U.S. Department of Housing and Urban Development (HUD), and the U.S. Office of Management and Budget (OMB). Then, we attach community area characteristics to each tax filer's record, including the median income relative to the area median income, urbanization, and concentration of bank establishments. For a detailed discussion of the data and methods we use in this report, see the description in the appendix.

Descriptive Analyses

Taxpayers who use RALs and RACs are not distributed randomly among the tax-filing population or the population of those receiving refunds. Relative to the average, they are more likely to display certain demographic and economic characteristics, geographical locations, timing of filing, and size of refunds. RAL and RAC recipients are much more likely to resemble each other than non-recipients, but there are still some modest differences between RAL and RAC users. We report on these key descriptors below and then explore how important certain characteristics remain when run through a multivariate model. While we examined taxpayer data from tax years 2005 to 2008, we only report the 2008 figures, as there was little change in use over this time (with one interesting exception relating to the military—described in subsequent pages).

Timing of Tax Filing. The filing of returns with refund anticipation loans and checks is overwhelmingly concentrated in the first few weeks of the tax season each year—a finding which speaks to the perceived need for quick credit on the part of these taxpayers. For tax year 2008 (where tax returns are filed mainly in January through April of calendar year 2009), over half of RACs were applied for by the third week in February; over 7 in 10 RACs have been applied for by the first week of March (figure 2). RALs are concentrated even earlier in the tax season. A remarkable 80 percent of RALs are applied for by the third week of February, and over 90 percent by the first week of March. The early submission of tax returns with RALs and RACs contrasts with other tax filers with refunds, only 16 percent of whom filed their taxes by the third week in February in TY 2008.

FIGURE 2: SHARE OF TAX RETURNS FILED BY DATE AND REFUND TYPE, TY 2008

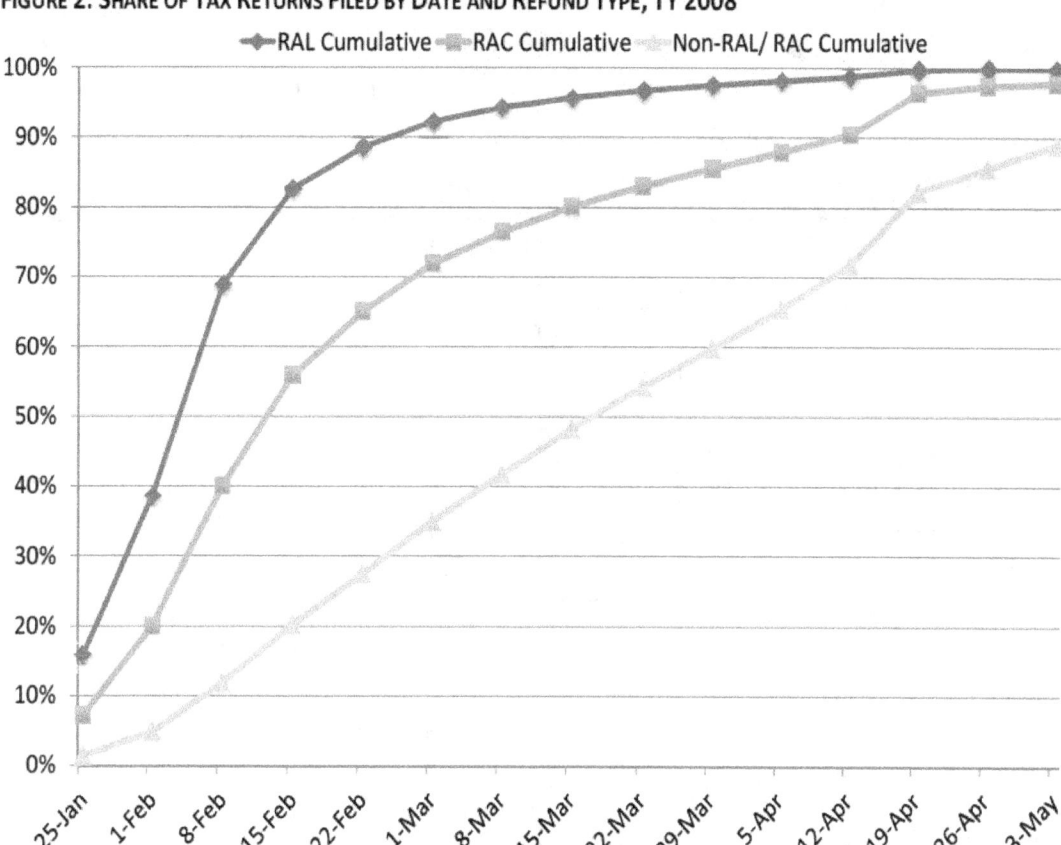

*Week the filing is posted to IRS's master administrative file.
Source: Authors' calculations of IRS taxpayer data.
Universe: All tax filers with a return.

Still, it is interesting to note that nearly 30 percent of RAC recipients wait to file their taxes until after the first week of March. This latter finding suggests that this subset of taxpayers does not need funds as quickly, and many (assuming they had the adequate information available) could have saved money simply by filing their taxes earlier and still receiving their refund at the same time or earlier than they did after paying for the advance refund.

Refund Amounts. RALs and RACs also differ from other tax returns in their size—RAL/RAC users tend to be concentrated more at higher refund amounts (although we didn't examine the breakdown among refund amounts above $5,000, where some high-income taxpayers might be found). The median refund amount for non-RAL/RAC users (with a refund) is $1,526, but for RAC recipients it is $2,703, and for RAL recipients, a sizable $3,577. Looking at the distribution, while 37 percent of non-RAL/RAC returns are for amounts less than $1,000, just 20 percent of RAC returns and 12 percent of RAL returns are below $1,000. Looking at the other end of the continuum, we see that 6 in 10 RAL recipients had a tax refund of over $3,000, while just 30 percent of non-RAL/RAC returns did. Again, RAC recipients fall between these two groups: 46 percent had returns worth over $3,000. These numbers confirm previous findings that RAL and RAC recipients typically receive large refunds, which are principally the result of refundable tax credits.

Table 3: Percent RAL, RAC, and Non-RAL/RAC Use by Refund Amount, TY 2008

Refund Amount	Share by Amount				Share by Product		
	RAL	RAC	Non-RAL/RAC	Total	RAL	RAC	Non-RAL/RAC
≤ $500	1%	4%	95%	100%	2%	7%	21%
>$500	5%	9%	86%	100%	10%	13%	17%
>$1,000	6%	10%	84%	100%	9%	11%	12%
>$1,500	6%	11%	83%	100%	7%	9%	9%
>$2,000	8%	12%	80%	100%	13%	14%	12%
>$3,000	12%	15%	73%	100%	16%	14%	9%
>$4,000	15%	16%	69%	100%	15%	12%	6%
>$5,000	13%	13%	74%	100%	28%	21%	15%
Total					100%	100%	100%

Source: Authors' calculations of IRS taxpayer data.

Preparer Type. Almost all RAL tax returns are recorded by the IRS as being prepared by paid preparers. This makes sense as RALs are loan products that require approval from a lender; this product is not available to self-preparers. However, the story with RACs is markedly different. Just 55 percent of RAC returns are prepared by paid preparers—comparable to the 57 percent of those without a RAL or a RAC who use paid preparers. While several brands of tax preparation software allow consumers to receive RACs, it is surprising to find RAC use so prevalent among self-prepared returns. The next section details the motives for RAL/RAC use according to paid preparers, but we do not have information on why taxpayers who self-prepare their returns choose RACs in such great numbers.

EITC Receipt. RALs and RACs usage by EITC recipients is higher than the population as a whole. The EITC is delivered through the tax code. Because it is difficult to know the amount of EITC to be received at the end of the year, most taxpayers receive just a single check after filing their returns, as opposed to receiving the money reflected over the year in withholding or through the Advance EITC program[3]. Due to the EITC and other refundable tax credits, some poorer households can receive close to $5,000 or as much as 40 percent of their income, with one check at tax time. Over 26 percent of EITC recipients with qualifying children take out a RAL and another 23 percent take out a RAC (table 4). Viewed from another angle, 64 percent of RALs and 42 percent of RACs are taken by EITC recipients. It is primarily EITC recipients with *qualifying children* who take out RALs and RACs—but EITC claimants without qualifying children generally are eligible for much smaller refund amounts.

---

[3] The Advance EITC was discontinued in 2010.

Table 4: Percent RAL, RAC, and Non-RAL/RAC Use by EITC Recipient Status, TY 2008

EITC Claim Status	Refund Type						
	Share by Status				Share by Product		
	RAL	RAC	Non-RAL/RAC	Total	RAL	RAC	Non-RAL/RAC
EITC Claimant w/ Qualifying Kid(s)	26%	23%	50%	100%	60%	38%	8%
EITC Claimant w/o Qualifying Kid(s)	7%	9%	84%	100%	4%	4%	4%
Non-EITC Claimant	3%	6%	91%	100%	36%	58%	88%
Total					100%	100%	100%

Source: Authors' calculations of IRS taxpayer data.

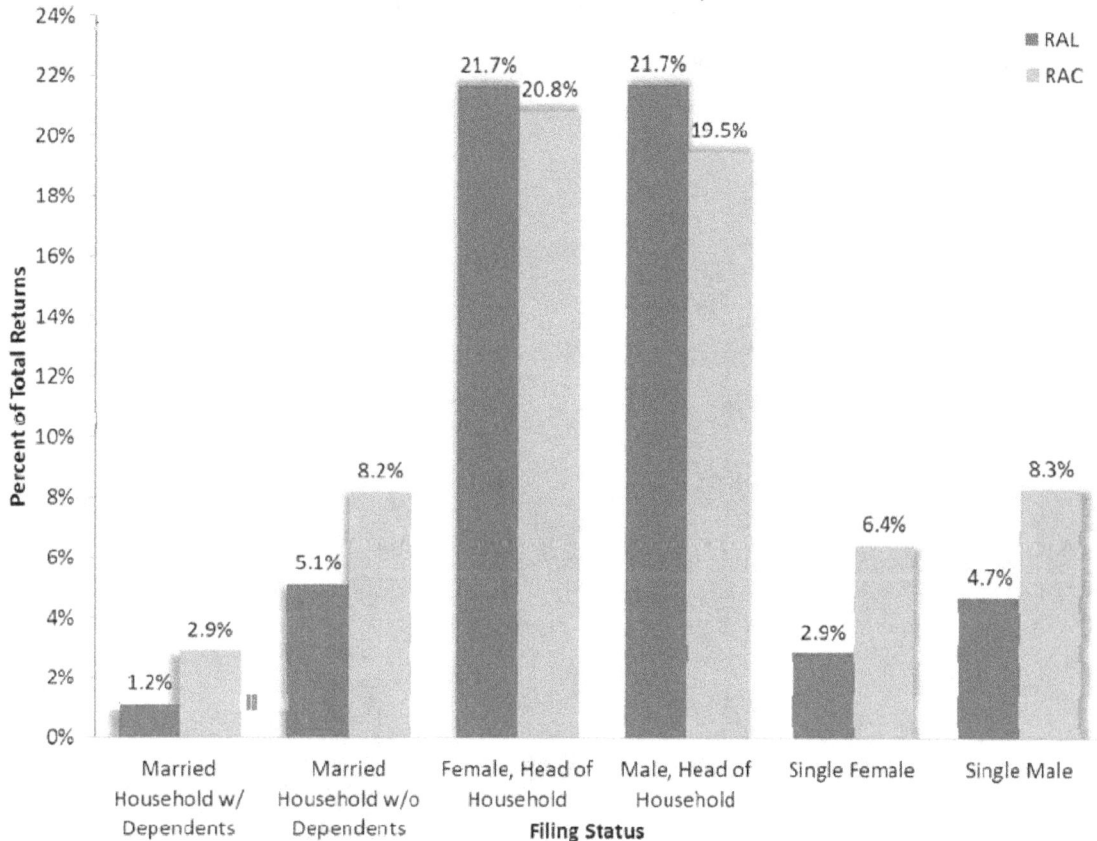

FIGURE 3: RAL AND RAC USE BY HOUSEHOLD FILING STATUS AND GENDER, TY 2008

Source: Authors' calculations of IRS taxpayer data.
Universe: All tax filers with a return.

Filing Status and Gender. If taxpayers are married, they will file their taxes jointly as a couple or in a smaller number of cases as "married filing separately." A single person living alone generally will file his or her taxes as a "single" return, while a single adult caring for one or more dependents will file as a head of household (HOH).

It is these HOH families that stand apart in their use of RALs and RACs (figure 3). Some 4 in 10 HOH filers received a RAL or RAC, split roughly evenly between the two products. Contrast that with married filers: fewer than 9 percent use a RAL/RAC. Single filers also use RALs and RACs at less than one-third the rate of HOH filers. RAC use was somewhat higher than RAL use for single and married filers. Interestingly, gender differences in use of RAL/RAC, once controlling for type of return, are only modest. What matters is whether the filer is parenting alone, not whether the filer is a man or a woman.

Presence of Children. Of course, most HOH filers have children and the presence of children is correlated with use of RALs and RACs. We explore the individual contributions of each characteristic in the multivariate analyses. Looking at descriptive figures, we see that tax filers with children present are bigger users of RALs and RACs than those without children. Over 12 percent of those with one or more children take out a RAL, compared with just 3.2 percent of those without children. Similarly, RAC use is higher among those with children (13.4 percent versus 6.1 percent for those without children).

FIGURE 4: RAL AND RAC USE BY AGE, TY 2008

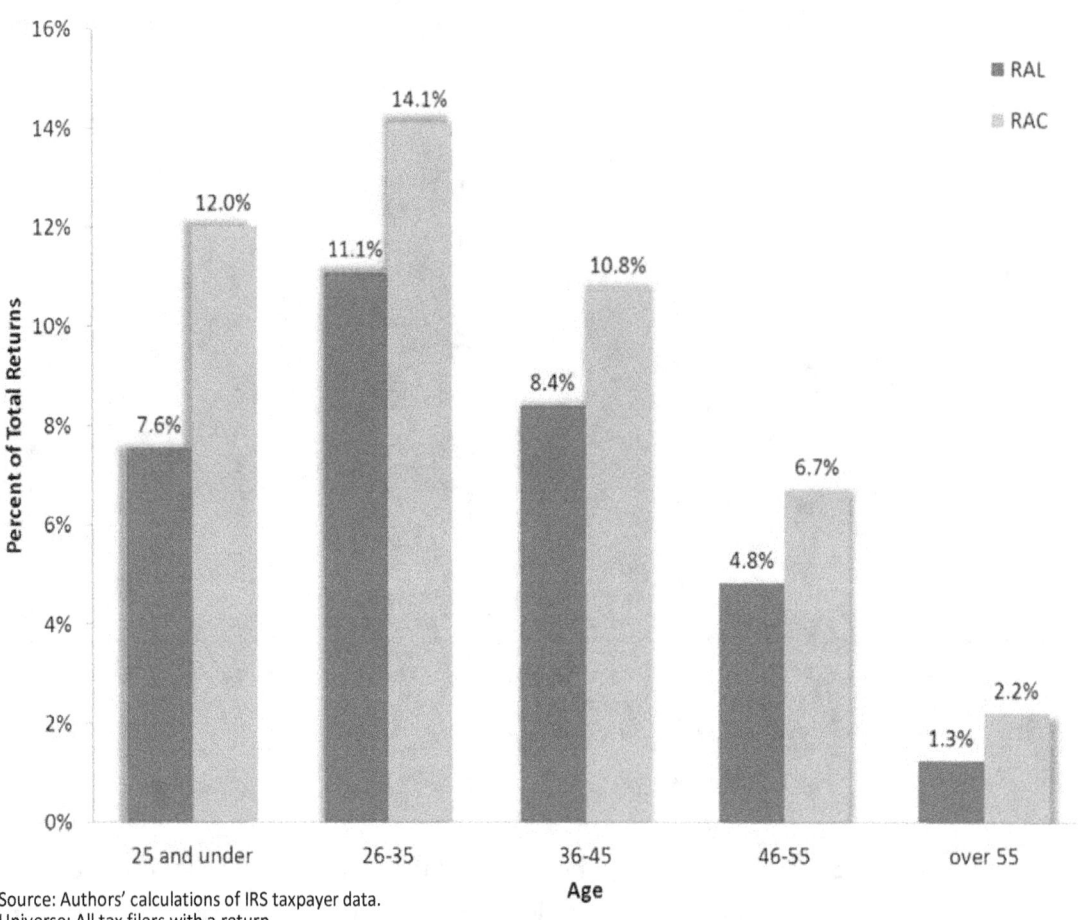

Source: Authors' calculations of IRS taxpayer data.
Universe: All tax filers with a return.

Age. The heaviest use of high-cost tax refund advances are by individuals and families in their early career years. The median age for RAL users is 34, the same as for RAC recipients. After age 45, the use of such products declines rapidly (figure 4). This is expected, as these are ages where tax filers generally have higher incomes and are less likely to have dependent children. Non RAL/RAC users are typically older: their median age is 45 years.

Service in the Armed Forces. IRS tax return data do not provide reliable information about the occupations of tax filers; however, primary and secondary taxpayers in the active armed forces can be identified using W-2 data. The military has for some time been concerned about its members becoming trapped in a cycle of high-cost small dollar debt, citing this as a threat to national security. The armed forces have, therefore, campaigned against auto title loans, payday loans, and other alternative financial products. In 2006, Congress passed the John Warner National Defense Authorization Act for Fiscal Year 2007, also referred to as the Military Lending Act, to protect military households (but not other families) from what it considered to be predatory lending practices. This act prohibits financial service providers from issuing loans with APRs of over 36 percent to members of the military and their dependents, including spouses and children under 18. Lenders face civil and criminal penalties for knowingly violating the Military Lending Act. (Code of Federal Regulations 2010, H.R. 5122 (2006)).

FIGURE 5: NUMBER AND TYPE OF RETURNS AMONG ACTIVE MILITARY TAXPAYERS, TY 2005 AND TY 2008

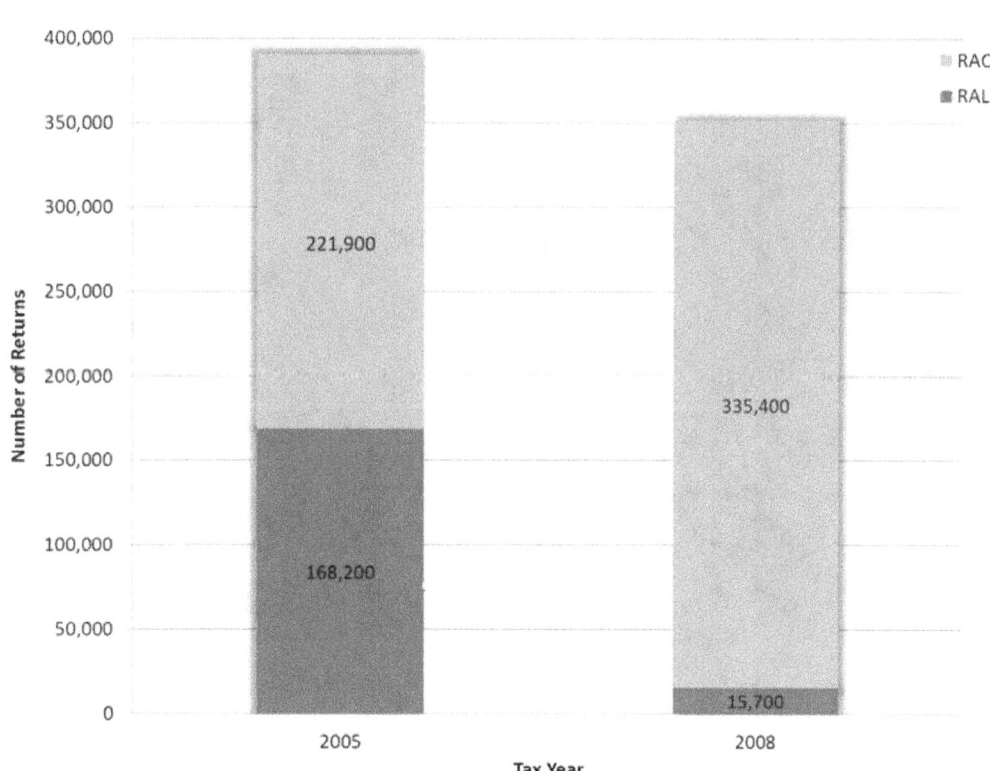

Source: Authors' calculations of IRS taxpayer data.
Universe: All tax filers with a return where the primary or secondary taxpayer was identified as an active military member and received a RAL or a RAC.

In 2005, before this legislation was passed, 168,200 members of the armed forces used a refund anticipation loan and another 221,900 used a RAC (figure 5). However, after instituting the APR cap, RAL use dropped precipitously, standing at 15,700 by 2008. Some, but not all, of these filers shifted to relatively lower-cost RACs; 335,400 took out a RAC in 2008. Unfortunately, there is little evidence of how these families fared as a result of this policy shift. For instance, did they alter their spending and savings habits? How much did the savings from not using a RAL mean to them?

Income. The heaviest use of RALs/RACs is among the working poor (figure 6). The median AGI among RAL users is $19,768. At the median, RACs are used by somewhat higher-income taxpayers: $24,072. Non-RAL/RAC users with refunds have AGIs of $36,858 at the median. Of tax filers earning $10,000–$25,000, one in four uses either a RAL or RAC. Those earning below $10,000 are not the biggest users of RALs and RACs; they do not have sufficient income to generate a sizable refund or receive the highest levels of EITC. Similarly, those with incomes above $50,000 often avoid these products, although, interestingly, a fair number of them use RACs.

FIGURE 6: RAL AND RAC USE BY INCOME, TY 2008

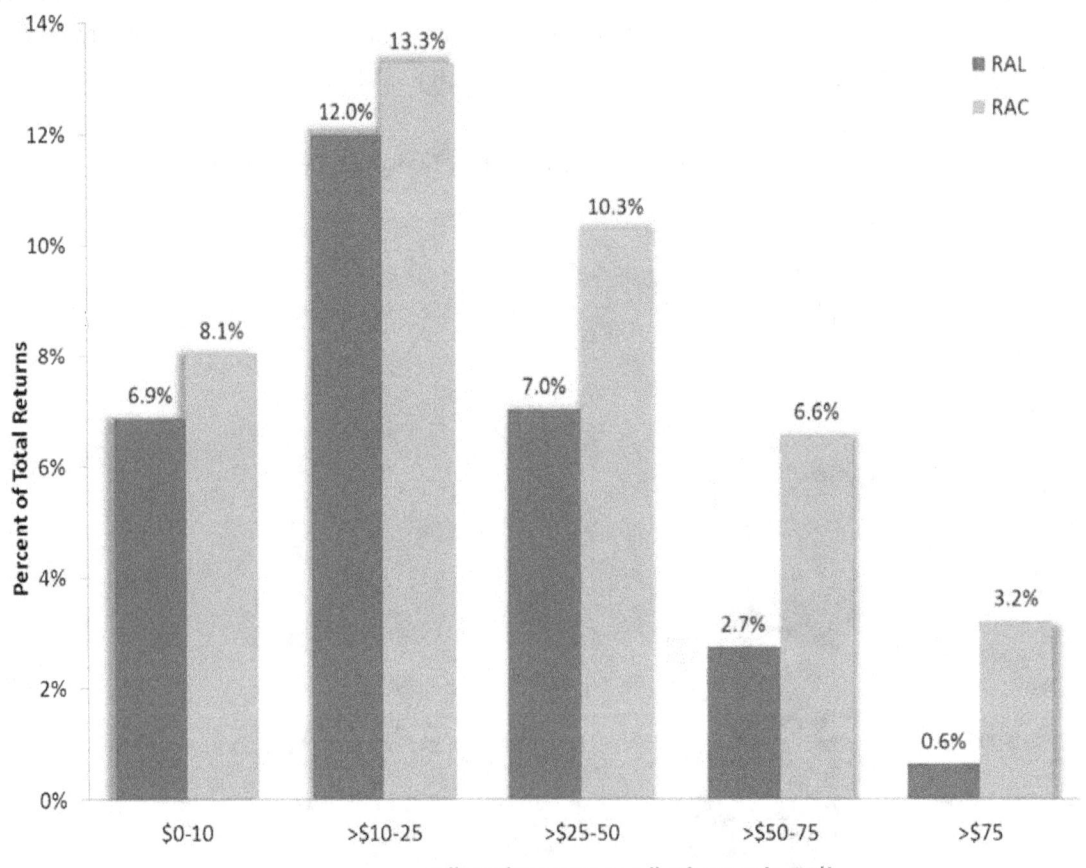

Source: Authors' calculations of IRS taxpayer data.
Universe: All tax filers with a return.

Asset Holding and the Unbanked. RAL/RAC use falls dramatically among households with interest or dividend income. We take the presence of interest and dividend income to be a proxy for banking status and at least some liquid assets, although some of the banked could be only in non-interest-bearing accounts. Assuming an interest rate of 2 percent, interest and dividend earnings of $50 would equate to savings of $2,500 and $250 to savings of $12,500. Those without any interest or dividend income are most likely to use RALs and RACs (25 percent use either a RAL or RAC). But just 7.2 percent of those with even low assets ($1–$49 in interest and dividend income) use a RAL or RAC. Tax filers with moderate savings ($50–$250 in interest and dividend income) rarely used RALs and RACs (4.5 percent) and just 1.3 percent of higher net worth individuals (greater than $250 in interest and dividend income) did. Generally speaking, almost any interest and dividend income corresponds to a dramatic drop off in use of these alternative financial products.

Geographic Concentration. RAL and RAC use is highly geographically concentrated. Research has not yet been able to determine why geographic concentration matters. There is some evidence that tax preparers have targeted low-income communities for their store placements (Rivlin 2010). Such targeting could be driven by economic factors. Or there could be particular cultural differences among communities, including different peer effects or proximity to stores. Whether this is driven by supply-side (tax preparer) or demand-side (taxpayers) motivations, or both, RALs and RACs are primarily received by taxpayers who live in poor communities, often of color. Given the income, racial, and other socioeconomic segregation in this country, this finding should perhaps not be surprising. But the degree of concentration is striking.

Figure 7 below shows RAL/RAC concentration by zip code, with a few communities (i.e. zip codes) contributing the bulk of RALs and RACs. Just 20 percent of all communities account for nearly 70 percent of all RALs and RACs.

One significant contribution from our research findings is the take-up of RALs and RACs at the zip code level. While research has aggregated RAL and RAC use at the state and national levels, we find interesting patterns of concentrated RAL and RAC use within states and across state zip codes. To display this concentration, we map the concentration of RAL/RAC use across the U.S. by zip code (figure 7). The diversity of RAL/RAC use is very evident.

FIGURE 7: PERCENT TOTAL RAL AND RAC USE BY PERCENT OF ZIP CODES, TY 2008

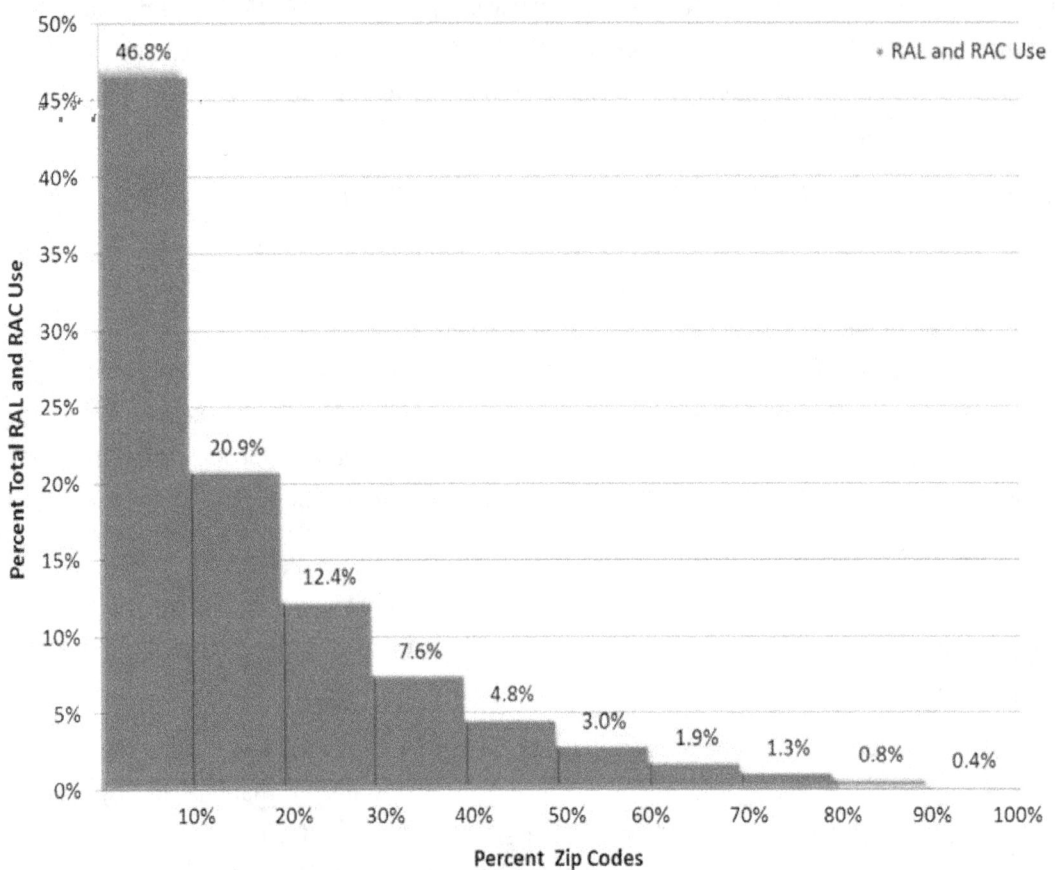

Source: Authors' calculations of IRS taxpayer data.
Universe: All tax filers with a return and living in zip codes with >10 RAL, RAC, or Non-RAL/RAC total returns; approximately 98 percent of tax filers with a return.

Communities in Appalachia and the Deep South have high rates of use, while many northern communities use RALs/RACs less frequently. Somewhat lost at this scale is the fact that high levels of RAL/RAC use are also prevalent in many cities, predominantly in the poorest communities, so we present RAL/RAC use from a few areas as illustrations. We find very different patterns of use across and within metropolitan areas such as Washington, D.C. and Chicago (figures 8 and 9). In these metropolitan statistical areas (MSAs), fewer than 5 percent of tax filers in many zip codes use RALs or RACs (combined). But there are also many communities where RAL/RAC returns represent more than 40 percent of all returns with refunds. In the supplemental appendix, we present tables documenting RAL/RAC use by state for the top 100 MSAs, and we also present select additional MSA-level maps of high, moderate, and low RAL/RAC-using areas.

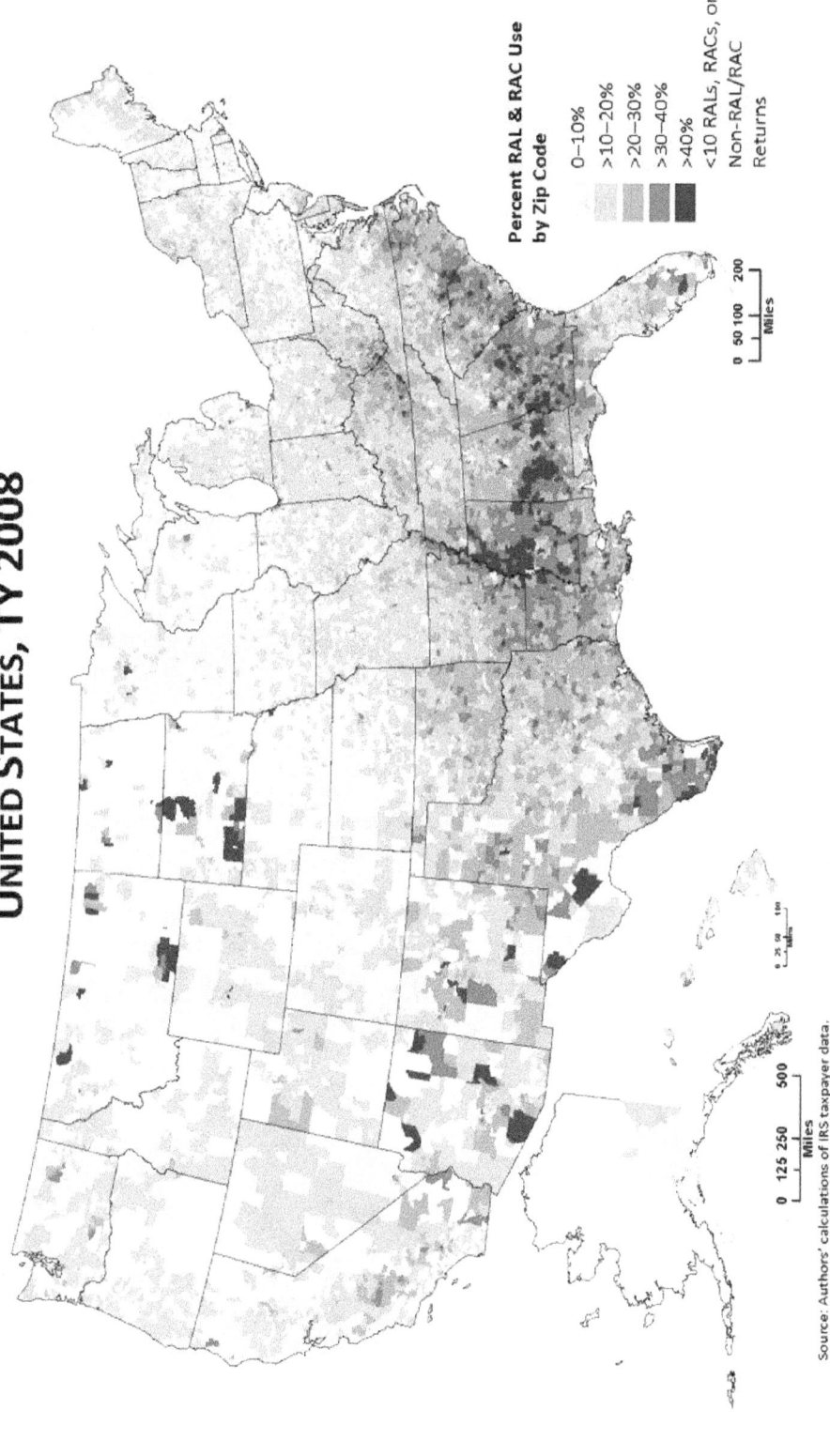

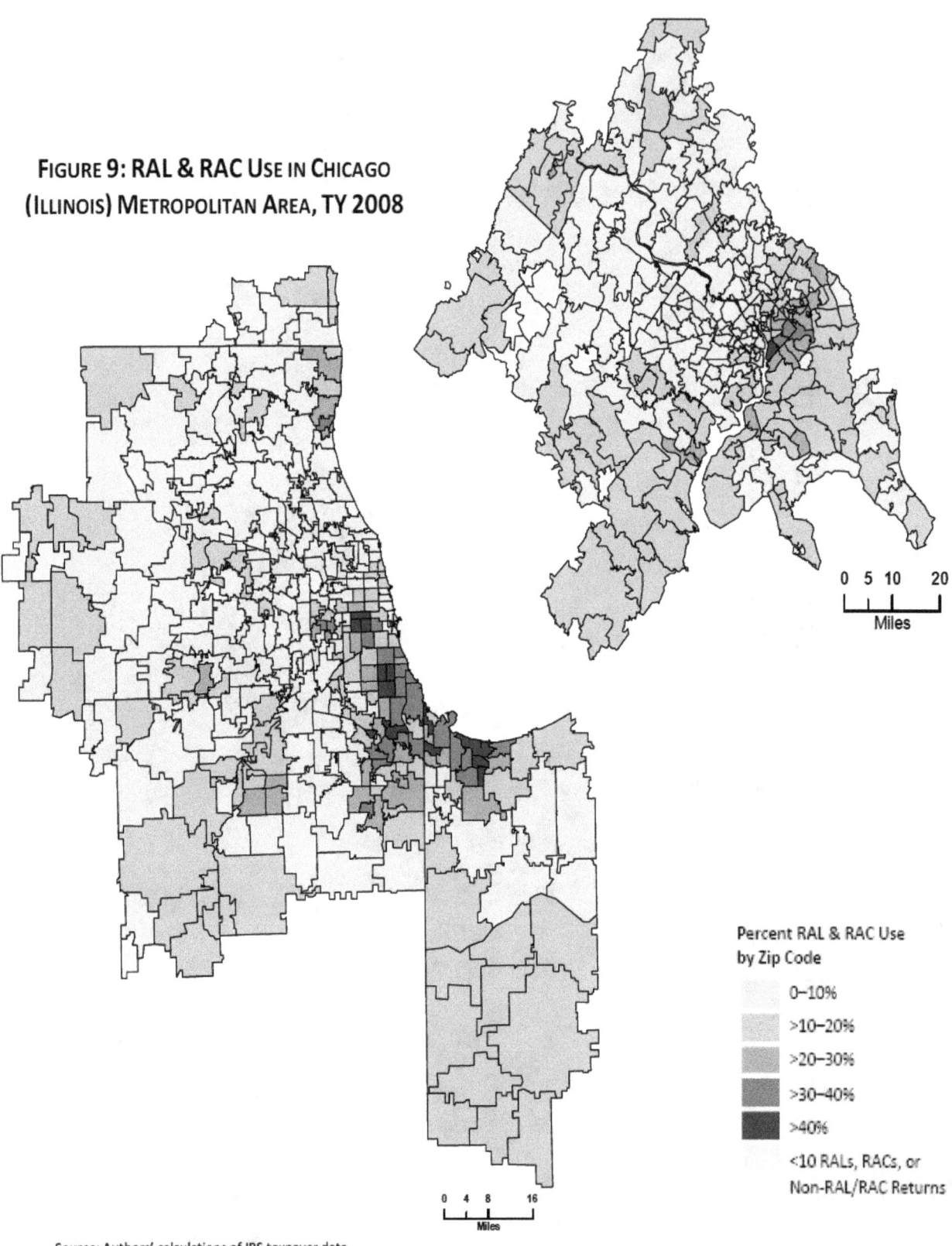

FIGURE 8: RAL & RAC USE IN WASHINGTON (DISTRICT OF COLUMBIA) METROPOLITAN AREA, TY 2008

FIGURE 9: RAL & RAC USE IN CHICAGO (ILLINOIS) METROPOLITAN AREA, TY 2008

Percent RAL & RAC Use by Zip Code
- 0–10%
- >10–20%
- >20–30%
- >30–40%
- >40%
- <10 RALs, RACs, or Non-RAL/RAC Returns

Source: Authors' calculations of IRS taxpayer data.
Universe: All tax filers with a return and living in zip codes with >10 RAL, RAC, or Non-RAL/RAC total returns; approximately 98 percent of tax filers with a return.

The Correlates of RAL/RAC Use

Multivariate models allow us to distinguish the relationship between each explanatory variable and RAL/RAC—for instance, whether RAL/RAC use is linked with low incomes or by the availability of EITC at different income levels. The goal of multivariate models is to distinguish the importance of each factor, while controlling for others. This model also allows us to understand how the explanatory variables' relationships to RAL and RAC use differ. In this study, we estimate a multinomial logistic regression model of the probability of use of a RAL, a RAC, or neither. Since we have such a large sample size, most of the explanatory variables are statistically significant. But what is of main interest here is the size of relationship of each variable to use of RALs and RACs, not merely its significance.

We describe these relationships by using odds ratios—that is, the percent increase or decrease of RAL or RAC use, after controlling for various characteristics. The "odds" of RAL use are defined as the relative probability of RAL use versus use of neither RAL nor RAC. The odds of RAC use are defined in a similar way. The odds ratio is a multiplier that provides a measure of how the odds are changed by being in a particular group, after controlling for various other characteristics. For categorical variables, this increase or decrease is in comparison with an omitted category, defined for each variable; we label these as reference groups. For example, from the RAL equation, the odds ratio for EITC without qualifying children is 1.95. This implies that the odds of receiving a RAL for those with EITC without qualifying children are 1.95 times the odds for those without EITC. This is equivalent to saying that they are 95 percent more likely for those with EITC without qualifying children as compared with those without EITC. We use the "likelihood" rather than "odds" nomenclature throughout, but define the term as described above. Additional output results are available in appendix table A.1.

Generally, the findings confirm the importance of variables where we saw differentials in the descriptive analyses. We find that many of the characteristics have even stronger associations with RAL take up than with RAC use. We explore the most important factors below.

EITC recipients have a much higher likelihood of using a RAL or a RAC especially if they have one or more qualifying children (figure 10). Compared with non-EITC claimants with or without qualifying children, EITC claimants with a qualifying child are over 125 percent more likely to use a RAL and over 75 percent more likely to take out a RAC compared to using neither product. The increase in likelihood, while still large, is slightly less for EITC recipients without qualifying children. They are 95 percent more likely to take out a RAL and 33 percent more likely to take out a RAC. This confirms descriptive findings on the higher use among EITC recipients and also provides insight into a predominant driver of RALs and RACs.

A taxpayer's refund amount has an important association with his or her decision to use a RAL or RAC. The higher a taxpayer's refund, the more likely he or she is to use a RAL or RAC. Relative to not using a RAL or RAC, for every 170 percent increase in refund amount, an individual is approximately 85 percent more likely to use a RAL and 45 percent more likely to use a RAC. Another way of saying this is that an individual with a refund amount of $1,360 has more than an 80 percent increased likelihood to use a RAL, or more than 40 percent increased likelihood of using a RAC, compared to an individual with a refund amount of $500.

FIGURE 10: PERCENT LIKELIHOOD OF RAL AND RAC USE BY EITC CLAIM STATUS

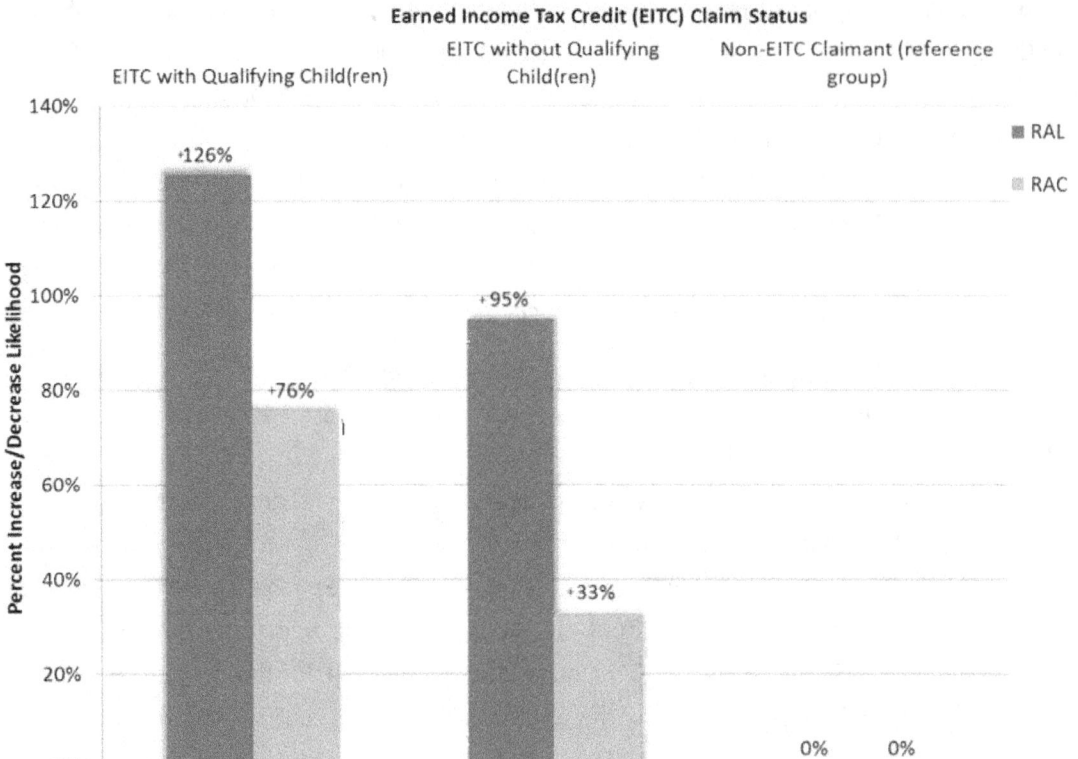

Source: Authors' calculations of IRS taxpayer data.
Universe: One percent random sample of all tax filers with a return.
Notes: The graph represents the increased/decreased probability of RAL/RAC use compared to the reference group. It depicts the graphed coefficients (odds ratios) resulting from the multinomial regression.

How taxpayers prepare their return is also significant. Relative to self-prepared returns, volunteer-prepared returns are 60 percent less likely to receive a RAC. Those who have their return prepared by a paid preparer are exponentially more likely to use a RAL or RAC than those who prepare their own returns. Indeed, RALs must be prepared by paid preparers, but 45 percent of RACs are taken out by taxpayers who prepare their own returns.

The increased likelihood of using a RAL or RAC varied by filing status but was most prominent among single-headed households with children (figure 11). Compared to households that are married and jointly file their tax return (and controlling for other factors), males and females who file their taxes as heads of households are about 160 percent and 130 percent more likely to take a RAL. Single-filing males and single-filing females (households without qualifying dependents) are also more likely to use RALs (85 percent for males and 26 percent for females). This suggests that gender is less important than the presence of children.

FIGURE 11: PERCENT LIKELIHOOD OF RAL AND RAC USE BY HOUSEHOLD FILING STATUS

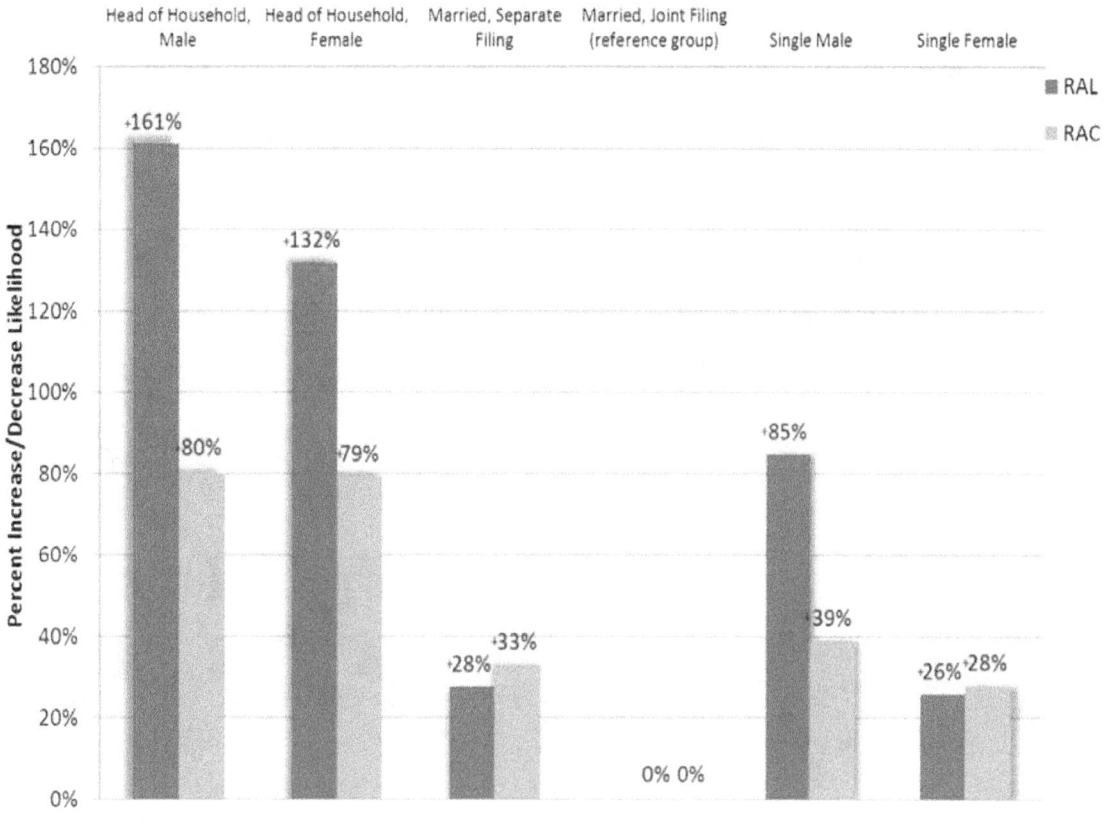

Source: Authors' calculations of IRS taxpayer data.
Universe: One percent random sample of all tax filers with a return.
Note: The graph represents the increased/decreased probability of RAL/RAC use compared to the reference group. It depicts the graphed coefficients (odds ratios) resulting from the multinomial regression.

Even after controlling for income and household filing status, older ages are associated with much lower use of RALs and RACs (figure 12). When compared to non-use of RALs/RACs, individuals who are younger than 34 years old are nearly 50 percent more likely to use a RAL or use a RAC compared to individuals in their middle ages, 45–54. The closer an individual is to retirement and old age, the less likely he or she is to use a RAL or RAC.

While many of the characteristics discussed thus far affect RAL and RAC use in the same direction, active military membership is associated with less RAL use and greater RAC use. Being an active military member is associated with an 85 percent decrease in the likelihood of RAL take-up but over a 100 percent increase in likelihood of RAC take-up. This demonstrates the power of the Military Lending Act, which prohibits military members from receiving loans with greater than 36 percent APR.

FIGURE 12: PERCENT LIKELIHOOD OF RAL AND RAC USE BY AGE

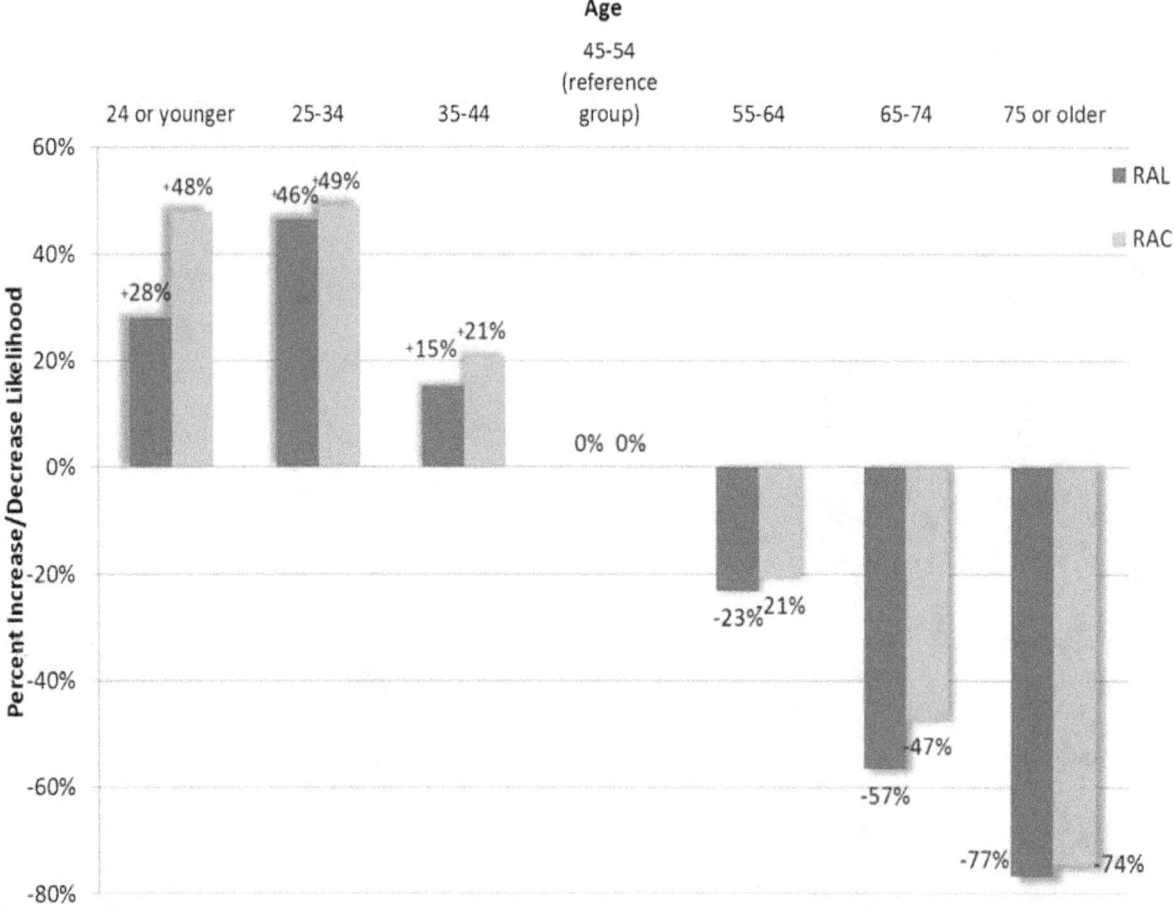

Source: Authors' calculations of IRS taxpayer data.
Universe: One percent random sample of all tax filers with a return.
Note: The graph represents the increased/decreased probability of RAL/RAC use compared to the reference group. It depicts the graphed coefficients (odds ratios) resulting from the multinomial regression.

We also find that low to moderate incomes, not just the lowest, are associated with higher use of RALs and RACs. Those earning less than $30,000–$35,000 (the omitted reference group) are 7 to 42 percent more likely to receive a RAL (table A.1). The association of income groups with RACs is nearly identical. Those earning above $45,000 are about 35 percent less likely to take up a RAL and RAC.

Even after controlling for income, we find that having earning assets—which can include simply being banked with some account that pays interest—matters (figure 13). Claimed interest and dividend income can act as a proxy for asset holdings. Having $1 in interest income could be the equivalent of having a $50 in a bank account with a 2 percent annual return. When compared to having no interest or dividend income, having any assets is related to decreases in RAL and RAC use; also, the more capital income an individual receives, the greater the decrease in likelihood of obtaining a RAL or RAC. It is likely that having assets lessens the need for RALs and RACs, for example, because the filer is able to pay the tax return preparation fees or has a bank account. But this measure likely conveys something more, as well, at least for some taxpayers. Those individuals who are banked—especially banked with interest-bearing accounts—operate in a different world of information, financial planning for the future, financial literacy, a greater personal tendency to save more and borrow less, ability to forestall consumption, easier ability to deposit refunds, lower amounts of other outstanding debts, or, most likely, some combination of all of the above.

FIGURE 13: PERCENT LIKELIHOOD OF RAL AND RAC USE BY INTEREST AND DIVIDEND INCOME

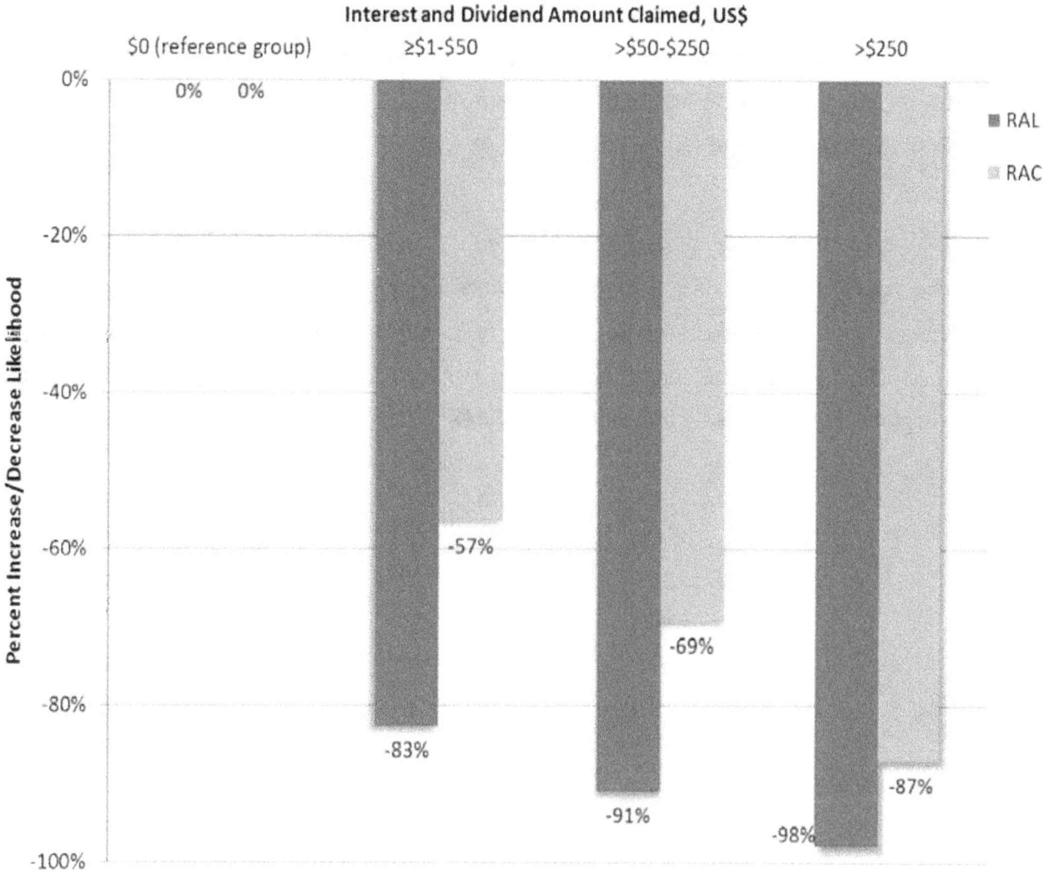

Interest and Dividend Amount Claimed, US$	RAL	RAC
$0 (reference group)	0%	0%
≥$1-$50	-83%	-57%
>$50-$250	-91%	-69%
>$250	-98%	-87%

Source: Authors' calculations of IRS taxpayer data.
Universe: One percent random sample of all tax filers with a return.
Note: The graph represents the increased/decreased probability of RAL/RAC use compared to the reference group. It depicts the graphed coefficients (odds ratios) resulting from the multinomial regression.

Geography matters profoundly. It is not the case that RAL/RAC use is simply explained by the characteristics of individual taxpayers. Geography can matter in several ways. First, RAL/RAC providers are concentrated in certain (poorer) communities, so geography reflects access to these financial products. Higher RAL/RAC use in certain zip codes may also reflect "peer effects," whereby potential RAL/RAC users are made aware of these products or encouraged to use them by neighbors, family, and friends. Given patterns of racial segregation, it is possible that higher use in certain areas reflects racial discrimination, a factor that has been demonstrated in other lending markets[4] but that we were not able to measure with this study. It is possible, finally, that geography captures other taxpayer-level characteristics that we were not able to include, like financial literacy, education, and English-language ability.

One of the strongest measures in our model is the relative affluence of a taxpayer's zip code. We create a ratio of the zip code's median income relative to the median income of the surrounding metropolitan area or county (for zip codes that are not part of an MSA). We then divide zip codes into five categories, extremely low-income areas (those whose median income is 0 to under 30 percent of area median income), very low-income areas (30 to less than 50 percent of AMI), low-income areas (50 to less than 80 percent of AMI), moderate income (80 to 120 percent of AMI), and upper income (over 120 percent of AMI).

As shown in figure 14 below, taxpayers living in extremely low-income communities are an astonishing 560 percent more likely to use RALs and 215 percent more likely to use RACS—controlling for their family characteristics and their income. Taxpayers in very low-income communities are 260 percent more likely to use RALs and 125 percent more likely to use RACs. Even taxpayers in low-income communities are significantly more likely to use RALs and RACs.

---

[4] See for example, Bates 1997; Blanchflower et al. 2003; Cohen-Cole 2008; Coleman 2002; Holloway and Wyly 2001; Schill and Wachter 1993; Squires 1997; and Turner et al. 2002.

FIGURE 14: PERCENT LIKELIHOOD OF RAL AND RAC USE BY AREA MEDIAN INCOME

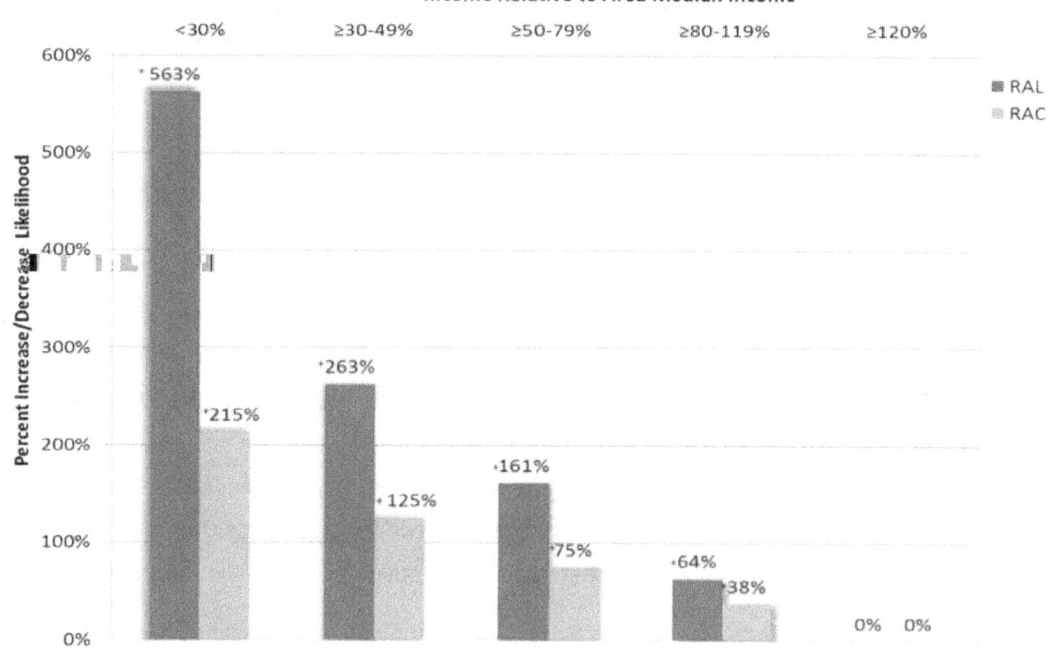

Source: Authors' calculations of IRS taxpayer data.
Universe: One percent random sample of all tax filers with a return.
Note: The graph represents the increased/decreased probability of RAL/RAC use compared to the reference group. It depicts the graphed coefficients (odds ratios) resulting from the multinomial regression.

After controlling for the income of the locality and the taxpayer-level characteristics, those living in rural areas are associated with higher levels of RAL and RAC use. An individual living in a densely populated area (super-urban) is nearly 70 percent less likely to use a RAL compared to individuals in rural areas. The association between urbanization and RAC take-up is weaker but still present—living in a densely populated area is related to nearly a 25 percent decrease in likelihood of RAC take-up.

When controlling for many individual-level and geographic-area variables, other community-level variables do not have important associations with RAL and RAC take-up. Though not presented here, additional models that include proxies to measure the effect of the education level, subprime mortgage activity, and unemployment level in the area where the individual lives do not demonstrate much association with RAL and RAC use. Living in an area with a high concentration of banks was associated with slightly lower uptake of RACs.

WHY TAXPAYERS USE RALS/RACS AND WHY TAX PREPARERS OFFER THEM

Our interviews with RAL/RAC industry stakeholders confirm that the number of RALs has been declining while the number of RACs has increased. However, stakeholders assert that a significant contingent of dedicated RAL users remains. The interviews largely supported the findings of past researchers into the motivations of RAL and RAC borrowers. Consistent with previous findings, industry respondents indicated that most RAL and RAC recipients use these products to pay for pressing financial obligations, both expected and unexpected, and for their tax preparation. RAL/RAC users, particularly those claiming the EITC, are driven to paid preparers by the complexity of filing a tax return. We also heard that some RAL/RAC recipients wanted this AFS product to access their refunds more quickly than they would otherwise be able to. Stakeholders from the RAL/RAC industry do not feel that consumers use these products because they fail to understand that they are loans or because they are not aware of the fees involved. Consumer advocates argue that use is partly driven by aggressive, targeted marketing.

While some past research has focused on consumer motivations for getting RALs or RACs, we could find no research addressing supplier motivation. The interviews conducted as part of this project begin to provide insights into supplier motivation, as well as industry perspectives on user motivations.

Data and Methods

We conducted qualitative interviews with 18 individuals at 11 different organizations, and they discussed topics ranging from product fees to motivations for RAL/RAC use and the future of the industry. The interviews also focused on RAL/RAC use associated with prepared returns. Those interviewed included conventional RAL lenders, tax preparers, low-cost RAL lenders, and VITA sites partnering with low-cost RAL lenders.

A sizable number of self-prepared returns also take RACs by using options available in tax preparation software (this option is not available for RALs). Since we did not interview or survey consumers in this study, our information on motivations is based mainly on the experiences of a range of industry stakeholders. Please see Methods and Data Appendix for a full description of the methods used to identify appropriate respondents and to conduct the interviews. This appendix includes a list of organizations that participated in the interviews.

Borrower Motivations

The interviewees largely confirmed our finding that the number of RALs has been declining in recent years while the number of RACs has increased. Stakeholders interviewed have seen the number of RAL clients decrease in absolute numbers and as a percentage of their business. In general, respondents report that customers seem to be increasingly willing to accept a wait of a few weeks to receive their funds rather than pay higher fees.

Although RAL use has declined in recent years, many dedicated users remain. Our interviews indicate that these borrowers use the products for many of the reasons identified by previous research. Industry stakeholders note that many individuals spend ahead or fail to make payments on rent, utilities, or other expenses during the holiday months with the expectation that they will receive a large lump sum in late January or early February. These are individuals for whom 10 days—the approximate time difference between receiving a RAL rather than a RAC—may be significant. RAL users also use the products because they do not have the cash on hand to pay for tax preparation fees. A majority of RAL users receive the EITC, and, according to our industry respondents, many feel that returns are too complex to complete by themselves. Last, some RAL recipients, both banked and unbanked, express mistrust of conventional financial institutions and use RALs as a way to receive their refunds while avoiding dealing directly with banks.

In many of these cases, one must also keep in mind the cost of alternatives. One industry commentator pointed out that the cost of a $3,000 RAL at about 2 percent would be cheaper than getting the same amount of money not only through other AFS products, but for many, even by borrowing on a credit card.

Quick Money to Alleviate Post-Holiday Financial Strain. According to the lenders, tax preparers, and others interviewed, RALs and RACs have become part of the annual financial cycle for some recipients. Their late fall and early winter spending habits reflect the knowledge that they will have a large influx of cash in late January or early February. Several respondents note that RAL and RAC users may leave utilities, rent, or car payments unpaid with the expectation that they will be able to pay them off at a certain time with a RAL or RAC. Recipients may also have seasonal work that has ended.

Consistent with the findings about an annual cycle, one stakeholder reports his organization has noted that its RAL users tend to fall into debt during the holiday months and see the RAL as a safe way to pull themselves out. The RAL amount is often enough to pay off the immediate debt (e.g., a car payment, mortgage or rent, or overdue utilities). He adds that his organization does not view the RAL as an ideal solution because it is not an asset-building tool, but he does see the loans as a useful means of paying off debts that might put recipients in an even more precarious financial position. Several stakeholders indicate that the windfall effect is very much in play, and that RAL recipients seem not to be sensitive to the associated fees, which some suggest are not that large relative to many other financial transactions.

General Financial Strain and Unexpected Expenses. In addition to holiday-related financial stress, respondents cite day-to-day financial obligations as a main reason consumers choose to take out RALs and RACs. Tax preparers and low-cost providers say that RAL/RAC customers are often in a financial crunch and that they are individuals with little or no disposable income who live day to day and who are often behind on bills. RAL users may have gotten an eviction notice, may need to make a payment on a car so they can drive to work, or may need to repair a car or an appliance.

All of the low-cost providers interviewed and a few of the conventional tax preparers interviewed say they make an effort to persuade customers to wait until their tax return is directly deposited or arrives in the mail or to take out a RAC instead of a RAL. In some cases, according to these respondents, these arguments are successful, but more often customers seem determined to get their funds quickly.

Lack of Funds to Pay for Tax Preparation Costs. An inability to pay for tax preparation is another commonly cited reason for receiving either a RAL or RAC, according to the interview respondents. One respondent estimates that at least 90 percent of those requesting RALs at his firm cannot pay for tax preparation fees. For the 2009 tax season, fees charged by H&R Block and Jackson Hewitt for tax preparation were approximately $187 (Wu and Fox 2010). For customers who are living paycheck to paycheck, this outlay may be more than they can afford, so they turn to a RAL or a RAC as a way to pay for tax preparation. In fact, as best as we could determine, often there were few other options. These customers could find a VITA site, although these are not available in all communities and some have limited hours of operation, or (if they have a bank account) turn to other potentially expensive alternatives such as payday loans to meet expenses.

Our interviews confirmed that a majority of RAL clients are EITC recipients, and some respondents argued that this is in part a result of aggressive marketing targeted at EITC claimants. Another respondent stated that the complicated instructions and forms for tax credits like the EITC are a major driver for the popularity of RALs and RACs. Many EITC recipients believe they need to use a tax preparer to file their taxes, and, unless they have access to free tax preparation at VITA sites, they may feel that the only way to pay the tax professional is to take the fees out of an advance refund.

Lack of a Bank Account. Stakeholders we interviewed report that many of their RAL/RAC customers are unbanked. Consumers without bank accounts who need cash quickly have limited choices. Direct deposit offers the fastest method for receiving a refund, but that requires a RAC or a RAL.[5] A refund issued by paper check takes longer to receive and, for the unbanked, may also involve a check-cashing fee. Also, the significant use of RACs on self-prepared returns appears related to the unwillingness or inability to pay these more modest fees with a credit card.

Mistrust of Conventional Financial Institutions. Interview respondents suggest that another reason consumers are attracted by RALs is that they allow people to borrow funds without coming into contact with a conventional financial institution. RAL and RAC customers may have bank accounts, but they may choose not to use them. Customers may have used the same tax preparer for several years and view the local tax preparation office as a friendly presence. On the other hand, banks may be seen as hostile. One VITA site operator who provides low-cost RALs through a bank with representatives on site says that his staff must make a concerted effort to ensure that clients feel comfortable because some inherent suspicion exists toward banks. Then, when customers are assured that the bank is providing them a service, they respond with gratitude, relief, and trust. Once those positive feelings are established,

---

[5] It should be noted that some RACs—for example, those offered through TurboTax in tax season 2010—require an existing bank account and are not available to the fully unbanked. That existing account can be a prepaid card rather than a traditional savings or checking account, and in some cases the card can be purchased when a filer is purchasing the RAC.

satisfied customers often respond by spreading the word among their friends and family about the program.

Military Families. Tax preparers interviewed have different views on the effect of the Military Lending Act on use of short-term credit among members of the military. One argues that the need for short-term credit has not diminished and that military households are turning to other forms of short-term credit. Another respondent believed that military households who used RALs in the past may well have changed their spending habits. She thinks the law has forced them to plan ahead and save in case unexpected expenses arise.

Supplier Motivations

Supplier motivations have not been explored extensively in past literature. A varied supplier market has evolved with a range of motivations expressed by the different providers we interviewed. Our interviews find that motivations for supplying RALs and RACs include profit, attracting customers to tax preparation businesses, providing financial education, and maintaining existing practices.

Commercial tax preparers that offer RALs and RACs indicate that they are in the market to meet demand for the product. Some argue that they must provide access to these products, since otherwise they would lose tax preparation business as well. Profits on the RALs and RACs are an obvious motivation for the presence of tax preparers in the market. Other stakeholders, such as software providers and lenders, also find RALs and RACs profitable.

Low-cost RAL program administrators indicate that they developed low-cost and free programs to respond to this consumer demand. These providers see the loans as a way to meet consumer demand, save consumers money that they might have spent on higher-cost loans and tax preparation, and offer financial education.[6]

Profit. RALs and RACs are profitable for the tax preparation firms, banks, and software intermediaries involved in the business.. Since industry stakeholders were understandably reticent about providing detailed information on profits, in this section we supplement our interview responses with secondary information. When HSBC stopped offering RALs through independent preparers because of reputational concerns, it was exiting a profitable business. According to a news report, Brendan McDonagh, CEO of HSBC North America Holdings, said the bank was giving up as much as $200 million in annual profits (Epstein 2009). SEC filings for Republic Bank & Trust Company, one of the few remaining RAL lenders and a publicly held company, indicate that RALs and RACs represent a major part of its business. For the

---

[6] The first low-cost RAL program was offered by Alternatives Federal Credit Union in Ithaca, New York, in 2002. The credit union has been providing low-cost loans, priced at $20 for tax season 2010, to keep their customers—and particularly low-income individuals and families who participate in the credit union's free tax assistance program—from going elsewhere for costly RALs. In the past few years, several nonprofits or city agencies that provide free tax preparation to low-income households through the IRS's VITA program have partnered with financial institutions to offer low-cost RALs, with fees ranging from free to $25. These programs can be found in Newark, New Jersey; Minneapolis, Minnesota; and San Antonio, Texas.

year ending December 31, 2009, net income from the company's tax refund business made up about 47 percent of the bank's total net income (Republic Bancorp Inc. 2009). In 2009, the net income for the bank's tax refund business was $20 million.

A representative of one RAL bank says that while RALs and RACs are profitable, profits vary by year due mainly to different loss rates. These losses arise from three areas. The first is that the IRS's debt indicator can be inaccurate, and the money lent to taxpayers cannot be recouped or recouped cheaply. As a result, there may be an unexpected offset to the refund. IRS revenue protection strategies may result in holding refunds, which can result in losses, as can fraud. RAL-providing banks spend a great deal of resources analyzing IRS funding patterns during the season, globally and at the office level, to mitigate risks in these areas. Another increasing cost over the past few seasons has been the cost of compliance and oversight.

Because RALs and RACs are profitable products, tax preparers and banks have an incentive to encourage the use of the products. In past years, these incentives took the form of payments to tax preparation firms or individual tax preparers, although such payments to individual preparers have been phased out in recent years, according to our interviews.

Bank products (RALs and RACs) are also profitable for the software companies/transmitters. Arrangements may vary, but one major software provider gets a fee for every bank product issued with its software. The fee is the same for RALs and RACs and does not vary with the size of the loan. Given the profit to be made from these products, it is not surprising that some transmitters encourage tax preparers to offer RALs and RACs. For example, CCH Small Firm Services, which publishes the widely used TaxWise software, offers free marketing material to TaxWise users touting bank products. CCH offers these promotional materials to "help TaxWise users get new clients in the door without the time and expense of creating their own marketing materials" (CCH Small Firm Services 2010).

Attracting Customers to Tax Preparation Businesses. Large and small tax preparation firms use RALs as a way to attract clients for their tax preparation services. One independent preparer interviewed notes that his firm would be pleased if RALs would disappear from the market. But as long as some tax preparation firms provide these sought-after products, his firm feels it must continue to offer them in order to remain competitive. One low-cost RAL provider reports that it began offering this product because their tax preparation operation was at a competitive disadvantage without a fast refund loan option.

Finally, the motivations of borrowers and lenders occur in a context that encourages the continuation of existing practices. RAL providers, whether they are for-profit or nonprofit, report that they are offering this service to meet the needs of those who feel they require a short-term loan at tax time.. While we have already noted some habit formation among taxpayers, the same may be true for individual tax preparers. For example, since half of EITC recipients use RALs and RACs, the preparer may simply become accustomed to diverting most EITC customers to RALs or RACs. Additionally, with repeat customers, it may be easy to pull out an old file and ask the customer if he or she wants the same services as last year.

Conclusion

By examining RAL/RAC use among tax returns, as well as through interviews with tax return preparers and other interested parties, we have been able to determine much more about who uses RALs and RACs and why. As expected, among the most important characteristics influencing RAL/RAC use were lower income, young adulthood, single head-of-household filing status, receipt of an EITC, and use of a paid preparer. In addition to giving more precision to the individual influence of each of these factors, we have also found other variables which significantly change the odds that people make use of RALs and RACs. Such variables include the presence of any interest or dividend income and living in poorer neighborhoods or in less urbanized areas (independently of one's own individual characteristics). Through interviews, we found evidence that some tax filers use RACs simply because they need to pay for tax return preparation—this is also true for individuals who make use of online software preparers.

REFERENCES

Bates, Timothy. 1997. "Unequal Access: Financial Institution Lending to Black and White-Owned Small Business Start-ups." Journal of Urban Affairs 19(4): 487-495.

Barr, Michael S. and Jane K. Dokko (2008). Third-Party Tax Administration: The Case of Low- and Moderate-Income Households. *Journal of Empirical Legal Studies,* 5:3, 963-981. December 2008.

Berube, Alan and Tracy Kornblatt (2005). "Step in the Right Direction: Recent Declines in Refund Loan Usage Among Low-Income Taxpayers." Washington, D.C.: The Brookings Institute.

Blanchflower, David G., Phillip B. Levine, and David J. Zimmerman. 2003. "Discrimination in the Small-Business Credit Market." The Review of Economics and Statistics 85(4): 930-943.

CCH Small Firm Services (2010). "Marketing Support." Accessed online at http://www.taxwise.com/resources/marketing.html on October 19, 2010.

Code of Federal Regulations (2010). "Title 32: National Defense, Part 232—Limitations on Terms of Consumer Credit Extended to Service Members and Dependents." Accessed online at http://ecfr.gpoaccess.gov/cgi/t/text/text-idx?c=ecfr&sid=2c63604480cfa5398069bcda6a693fbb&rgn=div5&view=text&node=32:2.1.1.1.29&idno=32 on October 14, 2010.Cohen-Cole, Ethan. 2008. "Credit Card Redlining." Federal Reserve Bank of Boston Working Paper No. QAU08-1.

Coleman, Susan. 2002. "The Borrowing Experience of Black and Hispanic-Owned Small Firms: Evidence from the 1998 Survey of Small Business Finances." Academy of Entrepreneurship Journal 8(1): 1-20.

Conference of State Bank Supervisors and American Council of State Savings Supervisors (2010). "CSBS/ACSSS Policy Position on High-Rate Refund Anticipation Loans." February 4, 2010.

Dewees, Sarah and Leslie Parrish (2008). "Borrowed Time: Use of Refund Anticipation Loans Among EITC Filers in Native American Communities." Longmont, CO: First Nations Development Institute.

Duda, Sarah, Katie Buitrago and Geoff Smith (2010). "Diverted Opportunity: Refund Anticipation Loans Drain Wealth from Low Wealth Tax Filers and Communities of Color." Chicago, IL: Woodstock Institute.

Eichenbaum, Peter, and Ryan Donmoyer (2010). "JPMorgan May Quit Tax-Refund Loans, Helping H&R Block." Bloomberg *Businessweek*. Accessed at http://www.businessweek.com on May 4, 2010.

Elliehausen, Gregory (2005). "Consumer Use of Tax Refund Anticipation Loans," Monograph #37. Washington, D.C.: Credit Research Center.

Epstein, Jonathan (2009). "HSBC Tries to Put Its House in Order: Focus Remains on U.S. Banking Business, While Consumer Finance Unit Is Scaled Back." *Buffalo News*, September 13, 2009.

Federal Deposit Insurance Corporation (2009). "National Survey of Unbanked and Underbanked Households." Washington, D.C.: Federal Deposit Insurance Corporation.

Feltner, Tom (2007). "Debt Detour: The Automobile Title Lending Industry in Illinois." Chicago, IL: Woodstock Institute and the Public Action Foundation.

FINRA Investor Education Foundation (2009). "Financial Capability in the United States Initial Report of Research Findings from the 2009 National Survey Component of the National Financial Capability Study." New York, NY.

Government Accountability Office (2009). "2009 Tax Filing Season: IRS Met Many 2009 Goals, but Telephone Access Remained Low, and Taxpayer Service and Enforcement Could Be Improved." Washington, DC: U.S. Government Accountability Office.

H.R. 5122 (2006). John Warner National Defense Authorization Act for Fiscal Year 2007. Accessed online at http://www.govtrack.us/congress/billtext.xpd?bill=h109-5122 on October 14, 2010.

H&R Block (2010). Exhibit 10.1 on Form 10-Q, filed with the U.S. Securities and Exchange Commission for quarter ending January 31, 2010. Accessed at http://investing.businessweek.com/research/stocks/financials/drawFiling.asp?docKey=137-000095012310022156-5DBR2S9C2E1MUUM7A5I084JNAN&docFormat=HTM&formType=10-Q#C56755EXV10W1_HTM on October 19, 2010.

Holloway, Steven R. and Elvin K. Wyly. 2001. "'The Color of Money' Expanded: Geographically Contingent Mortgage Lending in Atlanta." Journal of Housing Research 12(1):55-90.

Holt, Leonard (2009). Testimony by Leonard Holt, CCH Small Firm Services, at the IRS Return Preparer Review Forum, September 2009.

Internal Revenue Service (2009). "Return Preparer Review," Publication 4832. Washington, DC: Department of the Treasury, Internal Revenue Service.

Internal Revenue Service (2010a). "IRS Tax Topic 152: Refund Information." Accessed at http://www.irs.gov/taxtopics/tc152.html on August 11, 2010.

Internal Revenue Service (2010b). "Earned Income Credit (EIC): For Use in Preparing 2009 Returns," IRS Publication 596. Washington, DC: Department of the Treasury, Internal Revenue Service.

Johnson, Robert W. and D.P. Johnson (1998). "Pawnbroking in the U.S.: A Profile of Customers," Monograph # 34. Washington, D.C.: Credit Research Center.

Keeley, Chris, Sarah Ludwig and Mark Winston Griffith (2007). "Predatory Tax-Time Loans Strip $324 Million from New York City's Poorest Communities: An Analysis of Tax Refund Anticipation Lending in NYC 2002 – 2005." New York, NY: Neighborhood Economic Development Advocacy Project.

Liberty Tax Service (2010). "Investor Relations." Accessed at http://www.libertytax.com/investor-relations.html on September 19, 2010.

Masken, Karen, Mark Mazur, Joanne Meikle, and Roy Nord (2008). "Do Products Offering Expedited Refunds Increase Income Tax Non-Compliance?" Washington, D.C.: Office of Research, Analysis, and Statistics, Internal Revenue Service.

McKernan, Signe-Mary, Caroline Ratcliffe, and Daniel Kuehn. 2010. "Prohibitions, Price Caps, and Disclosure Policies: A Look at State Policies and Alternative Financial Product Use" Final report prepared for U.S. Department of the Treasury. Washington, D.C.: The Urban Institute.

Nelson, Brett, and Maureen Farrell (2010). "The Most Profitable Small Businesses." *Forbes*, April 15, 2010.

Nish, Caitlin (2010). "H&R Block: Refund Program at Risk." *Wall Street Journal.* October 19, 2010.

Office of the Comptroller of the Currency (2010). "Policy Statement on Tax Refund-Related Products." Accessed at http://www.occ.treas.gov/ftp/bulletin/2010-7.html on September 20, 2010.

Republic Bancorp Inc. (2009). Form 10K: Annual Report for fiscal year ended December 31, 2009. Filed with the United States Securities and Exchange Commission.

Rivlin, Gary (2010). B*roke, USA: From Pawnshops to Poverty, Inc. How the Working Poor Became Big Business*. New York, NY: Harper Collins.

Schill, Michael H. and Susan M. Wachter. 1993. "A Tale of Two Cities: Racial and Ethnic Geographic Disparities in Home Mortgage Lending in Boston and Philadelphia." Fannie Mae Journal of Housing Research 4(2):245-275.

Skiba, Paige Marta and Tobacman, Jeremy Bruce (2009). "Do Payday Loans Cause Bankruptcy?" Accessed at law.vanderbilt.edu/faculty/faculty-personal-sites/paige-skiba/download.aspx?id=2221 on December 7, 2009).

Squires, Gregory D. 1997. Insurance Redlining: Disinvestment, Reinvestment, and the Evolving Role of Financial Institutions. Washington, DC: Urban Institute Press.

Streitfeld, David, and John Collins Rudolph (2009). "State Are Pondering Fraud Suits against Banks." *New York Times*, November 3, 2009.

Tax Analysts (2010). "Daily Tax Highlights and Documents." Accessed at http://www.taxanalysts.com on September 25, 2010.

Treasury Inspector General for Tax Administration (2008). "Many Taxpayers Who Obtain Refund Anticipation Loans Could Benefit From Free Tax Preparation Services." Washington, D.C.: Department of the Treasury.

Turner, Margery A., Fred Freiberg, Erin Godfrey, Carla Herbig, Diane K. Levy, and Robin R. Smith. 2002. "All Other Things Being Equal: A Paired Testing Study of Mortgage Lending Institutions." Washington, DC: The Urban Institute.

WebCPA (2010). "Jackson Hewitt Strikes RAL Deal with Republic." Accessed at http://www.webcpa.com/news/ on March 30, 2010.

Wu, Chi Chi (2005). "Corporate Welfare for the RAL Industry: The Debt Indicator, IRS Subsidy, and Tax Fraud." Boston: National Consumer Law Center.

Wu, Chi Chi, and Jean Ann Fox (2010). "Major Changes in the Quick Tax Refund Loan Industry." NCLC/CFA 2010 Refund Anticipation Loan Report. Boston: National Consumer Law Center.

METHODS AND DATA APPENDIX

IRS Administrative and Secondary Data

This section describes the quantitative data and methods we use to inform our research questions. A joint effort by researchers at the Urban Institute and IRS Office of Research allowed us to make estimates on the basis of a large number of individual tax returns, while protecting taxpayers' confidentiality. For this research, the IRS shared aggregate statistics—not individual-level taxpayer data—with Urban Institute researchers. The IRS only provided data on subgroups with sample sizes large enough to prevent any ability to decipher taxpayer-level information.

Descriptive Analyses

IRS tax return data provide a rich source of information to document RAL and RAC use and correlate it with individual- and geographic-level characteristics. Using data from tax years 2005–2008, we ran descriptive analyses on the universe of tax filers 18 years or older with refunds. We excluded tax filers who did not receive a refund as they could not take out a RAL or RAC. Out of 136 million tax filers over 17 years old in 2008, 111 million received a refund from the IRS. In TY 2007, 105 million taxpayers received a refund; 106 million did in TY 2006, and 100 million did in TY 2005. Additionally, it is important to note that our unit of analysis, tax filers, does not always equate to households or families as they are conventionally defined, as these may be composed of multiple tax filers. We report findings almost exclusively for tax year 2008, as there were few differences in the characteristics of RAL and RAC users in prior years.

The factors included in our descriptive analyses are receipt of a RAL/RAC, refund amount, date of tax filing, EITC claim status, tax-filing status and gender, children present in the household, age, adjusted gross income, interest and dividend income, active military membership (for the primary or secondary tax filer), and return preparation type (paid preparer, volunteer preparer, or self-prepared). The IRS does not collect information on other qualities of interest, for example, education levels, occupations, race/ethnicity, and nativity, so our analysis cannot explore patterns of RAL and RAC use by these characteristics at the taxpayer level.

For descriptive geographic analyses, the IRS excluded zip codes where fewer than 10 returns were received in any of the return type categories (RAL, RAC, and non-RAL/RAC) due to disclosure concerns. Beyond this limitation, we were able to use zip code information to describe the concentration of RALs and RACs within zip codes and map their prevalence.

Multivariate Analysis

To isolate the influence of individual factors on the decision to take up a RAL or RAC, we ran a multivariate regression. While the descriptive analyses are informative, they do not allow us to interpret the influence of any explanatory variable in isolation, as many of these variables are correlated. We created a 1 percent simple random sample of U.S. taxpayers in TY 2008 and TY 2005 to use for the multivariate analysis. As with the descriptive analyses, we only report results from TY 2008 as the findings for the two years were nearly identical.

We ran a multinomial logistic regression, which allows for two or more categories for our dependent variable and assumes that there is no predictable ordering of the outcomes in question. The categories are: receiving a RAL, receiving a RAC, or receiving neither. Not receiving a RAL/RAC is the omitted category. We include as predictors only variables that we expect will influence the decision to take up a refund anticipation loan or check. These include several taxpayer-level characteristics as well as secondary data about the communities where taxpayers live. We ran the procedure in SAS using the surveylogistic procedure. The standard errors account for any clustering by zip code.

The taxpayer-level factors in our analyses are all drawn from the tax administration records. Their specifications are described below:

- RAL/RAC use. This is based on what the preparer (self, volunteer, or paid) reported on the tax return.

- Refund amount. We include the natural log of the taxpayer's refund amount.

- EITC claim status. We include two separate dummy variables, EITC with qualifying children and EITC without qualifying children. Omitted is the third option, not receiving the EITC.

- Tax-filing status. There are six potential filing statuses: female head of household, male head of household, female filing singly, male filing singly, married filing jointly, and married filing separate. We include five dummy variables, with omitting married filing jointly as the reference group.

- Claiming dependent children living at home. We include dummy variables for whether a taxpayer claimed 1, 2, or 3 or more dependent children, omitting the category "no dependent children living at home claimed."

- Age. As the influence of age on RAL/RAC receipt may not be linear, we include age categories (below 24, 25–34, 35–44, 55–64, 65–74, and over 75). We omit the age category 44–54 as the reference group.

- AGI. Similarly, we include information about AGI as categories, rather than as a continuous variable. The categories run from $0 to $45,000 in increments of $5,000, with AGIs above $45,000 grouped into one category. We omit the category for those earning from $30,000 to $35,000.

- Interest and dividend income. We create four categories of interest and dividend income: $0, $1.00–$50.00, $50.01–$250.00, and greater than $250.01, with no interest and dividend income as the reference group.

- Unemployment compensation. This dummy variable indicates those taxpayers who report any unemployment compensation.

- Active military member. This dummy variable indicates whether the primary or secondary taxpayer is an active member of the military.

- Preparer type. Taxpayers can prepare their tax forms personally (self-prepared) or have them prepared by a volunteer or paid preparer. We include two variables for preparer status (volunteer preparer, paid preparer) and omit self-preparers as the reference group.

Along with these individual characteristics, we include information about where taxpayers live, which may help to explain their use of RALs and RACs. We assemble geographic information from HUD, FDIC, and OMB, and merge this onto the tax filer–level records.

- Median income of zip code relative to area median income. This is a measure of the relative poverty or affluence of a community. For every zip code, we calculate the ratio of its median income (taken from IRS tax returns) over the median income for the surrounding area (from HUD). For zip codes in metropolitan areas, we use the metropolitan statistical area's median income; for zip codes not in metropolitan areas, we use the county's median income. We create five categories of this ratio: zip codes where median income is 0–<30 percent of the area median, 30–<50 percent, 50–<80 percent, 80–<120 percent, and >120 percent. We omit the last category in the regression analyses.

- Urbanization. OMB created an assessment of how urban or rural counties are, and we use these definitions here. A county can be defined as super-urban, urban, suburban, or rural. We omit the rural category as a reference group.

- Bank concentration. With data from the FDIC, we calculate the number of bank branches per 10,000 people (at the county level). We include this as a percent.

The point estimate and p-value from our multivariate analysis output is shown in table A.1.

Table A.1: Odds Ratio and P-Values

Variable	RAL Point Estimate	RAL P-Value	RAC Point Estimate	RAC P-Value
Natural Log of Refund Amount	1.846	<.0001	1.434	<.0001
Head of Household, Female	2.319	<.0001	1.792	<.0001
Head of Household, Male	2.614	<.0001	1.802	<.0001
Married, Filing Separately	1.276	<.0001	1.330	<.0001
Single Female	1.259	<.0001	1.280	<.0001
Single Male	1.846	<.0001	1.390	<.0001
EITC w/o Qualifying Child(ren)	1.951	<.0001	1.330	<.0001
EITC w/ Qualifying Child(ren)	2.257	<.0001	1.756	<.0001
Household w/ 1 Dependent	0.952	0.0019	1.017	0.1898
Household w/ 2 Dependents	1.087	<.0001	1.048	0.0006
Household w/ 3+ Dependents	1.111	<.0001	0.983	0.3269
Age 24 or Younger	1.282	<.0001	1.475	<.0001
Age 25–34	1.464	<.0001	1.491	<.0001
Age 35–44	1.153	<.0001	1.209	<.0001
Age 55–64	0.768	<.0001	0.792	<.0001
Age 65–74	0.435	<.0001	0.529	<.0001
Age 75 or older	0.234	<.0001	0.257	<.0001
AGI ≤ $5,000	1.369	<.0001	0.858	<.0001
AGI > $5,000–$10,000	1.468	<.0001	1.165	<.0001
AGI > $10,000–$15,000	1.232	<.0001	1.186	<.0001
AGI > $15,000–$20,000	1.276	<.0001	1.087	<.0001
AGI > $20,000–$25,000	1.179	<.0001	1.032	0.0728
AGI >$25,000–$30,000	1.075	0.0013	0.967	0.0602
AGI > $35,000–$40,000	1.044	0.0957	1.046	0.0249
AGI >$40,000–$45,000	1.089	0.0029	1.111	<.0001
AGI >$45,000	0.645	<.0001	0.939	0.0002
Interest and Dividends ≥$1–$50	0.173	<.0001	0.434	<.0001
Interest and Dividends >$50–$250	0.091	<.0001	0.307	<.0001
Interest and Dividends >$250	0.021	<.0001	0.130	<.0001
Unemployment Compensation	1.190	<.0001	1.105	<.0001
Active Military	0.171	<.0001	2.091	<.0001
Paid Preparer	58.427	<.0001	1.895	<.0001
Volunteer Preparer	0.394	<.0001	0.005	<.0001
AMI <0%	6.626	<.0001	3.147	<.0001
AMI ≥30–49%	3.627	<.0001	2.254	<.0001
AMI ≥50–79%	2.611	<.0001	1.748	<.0001
AMI ≥80%	1.638	0.0003	1.380	0.0015
Suburban Zip Code (≥500–2,499)	0.709	<.0001	0.995	0.6984
Urban Zip Code (≥2,500–7,499)	0.557	<.0001	0.892	<.0001
Super-Urban Zip Code (≥7,500)	0.315	<.0001	0.746	<.0001
Bank Concentration	0.994	0.3194	0.953	<.0001

Insights from Stakeholders

To complement our analysis of IRS data on RAL/RAC use, we conducted interviews with conventional RAL lenders, tax preparers, low-cost RAL lenders, VITA sites partnering with low-cost RAL lenders, and consumer advocates. We interviewed 18 individuals at 11 organizations, both over the telephone and in person. The list of potential interviewees was compiled after a review of RAL/RAC literature, web research, and exploratory interviews with five individuals actively or formerly involved in the RAL/RAC industry as providers, advocates, or regulators. The contacts at the major tax preparation firms and major RAL lenders were recommended by those we interviewed. The low-cost RAL providers and VITA sites were identified through our literature and web research. The contacts at independent tax preparation businesses were active in an online industry discussion group where they commented extensively and knowledgeably on the subject of RALs and RACs. The interviews ranged from about 20 minutes to one hour.

We made certain to interview at least one representative from each of the five groups we were interested in: conventional RAL lenders, tax preparers, low-cost RAL lenders, VITA sites partnering with low-cost RAL lenders, and consumer advocates. We interviewed four individuals at two RAL lenders, two individuals at an independent tax preparation firm, two individuals either currently or formerly employed by a major tax preparation chain, five individuals working at three VITA sites partnering with a low-cost RAL lender, two individuals working at a low-cost RAL lender, one representative from a transmission software firm, and two consumer advocates. We did not interview individual taxpayers. Most of the individuals whom we initially contacted agreed to be interviewed.

Questions varied based on what part of the RAL/RAC industry the respondent represented. Tax preparation chains and independent preparers were asked about business operations (fees, operating procedures, advertising, etc.), customer characteristics, and the reasons given for taking out the products. Some of these respondents also were asked for an assessment of the future of the RAL/RAC market. The interview with the transmission software firm focused on how the software works, fee structures, and the future of the market. Questions for conventional lenders touched on profits and risks, changes within the market, and alternatives to conventional RAL/RAC products. Low-cost providers addressed some of these same questions, as well as questions about their partnerships with VITA sites, how their practices compare to conventional RAL lenders, and the scalability of their models. VITA sites commented on the history and mechanics of their partnerships with low-cost lenders, program requirements and outcomes, and views on the how the partnerships could be sustained or scaled up. Questions for consumer advocates focused on the characteristics of RAL/RAC users, marketing of tax-time loan products, and alternatives to conventional RALs and RACs.

We spoke with the following organizations:

- Accountability Minnesota
- Alternatives Federal Credit Union (Ithaca, New York)
- CCH Small Firm Services

- City of San Antonio VITA Site, Department of Community Initiatives, Office of Financial Empowerment
- H&R Block
- NM&P Consulting
- National Community Tax Coalition
- Newark Now
- Peoples Income Tax Inc. (Richmond, Virginia)
- Republic Bank & Trust Company
- Santa Barbara Tax Products Group

SUPPLEMENTAL APPENDIX

Table B.1: Percent RAL, RAC, and Non-RAL/RAC Use by State, TY 2008

State	Refund Type			
	RAL	RAC	Non-RAL/RAC	Total
Puerto Rico	27.5	4.8	67.7	100
Mississippi	16.5	14.3	69.2	100
Louisiana	12.4	14.1	73.5	100
Alabama	12.5	12.4	75.1	100
Georgia	9.4	14.1	76.5	100
South Carolina	12.0	10.2	77.8	100
Arkansas	12.4	9.6	78.0	100
Texas	9.5	11.5	79.0	100
North Carolina	10.2	10.7	79.1	100
Tennessee	10.5	8.7	80.8	100
Kentucky	10.2	8.7	81.1	100
Oklahoma	8.9	9.7	81.4	100
West Virginia	9.2	8.4	82.4	100
New Mexico	7.1	10.1	82.8	100
District of Columbia	6.5	10.5	83.1	100
Nevada	7.8	9.0	83.1	100
Arizona	5.8	10.3	83.9	100
Indiana	7.4	8.4	84.2	100
Florida	6.3	9.4	84.3	100
Delaware	5.5	8.8	85.7	100
Missouri	6.5	7.8	85.7	100
Virginia	5.6	8.6	85.8	100
Ohio	6.2	7.5	86.4	100
Rhode Island	5.1	8.4	86.5	100
Michigan	5.2	8.2	86.6	100
Illinois	5.3	8.1	86.6	100
Maryland	4.3	9.0	86.7	100
New York	4.5	8.1	87.4	100
Kansas	5.0	7.4	87.6	100
Wyoming	6.0	6.4	87.7	100
Idaho	4.1	8.2	87.8	100
Hawaii	4.0	8.1	87.9	100
New Jersey	4.3	7.4	88.3	100

Table B.1: Percent RAL, RAC, and Non-RAL/RAC Use by State, TY 2008

State	Refund Type			
	RAL	RAC	Non-RAL/RAC	Total
Pennsylvania	4.6	7.0	88.4	100
Utah	4.1	7.5	88.5	100
Montana	5.0	6.4	88.5	100
Colorado	3.8	7.6	88.6	100
Nebraska	4.1	7.1	88.8	100
Alaska	4.4	6.8	88.8	100
California	3.8	7.4	88.8	100
South Dakota	6.2	4.8	88.9	100
Maine	3.9	6.6	89.5	100
Iowa	4.2	6.1	89.7	100
Connecticut	3.5	6.8	89.7	100
Other*	0.1	10.1	89.8	100
Washington	4.2	5.8	90.0	100
Oregon	3.0	6.8	90.2	100
Vermont	3.2	6.0	90.8	100
North Dakota	4.0	5.1	90.9	100
Wisconsin	2.9	6.1	91.0	100
New Hampshire	3.5	5.3	91.2	100
Massachusetts	2.6	6.1	91.3	100
Minnesota	2.2	5.0	92.8	100
Total	6.2	8.6	85.3	100

*Includes Armed Forces Americas (except Canada), Armed Forces Africa, American Samoa, Federated States of Micronesia, Guam, Marshal Islands, Northern Mariana Islands, Palau, U.S. Virgin Islands
Source: Authors' calculations of IRS taxpayer data.
Universe: All tax filers with a return.

Table B.2: Percent RAL, RAC, and Non-RAL/RAC Use by Metropolitan Statistical Area, TY 2008

State(s)	Metropolitan Statistical Area	RAL	RAC	Non-RAL/RAC	Total
TX	McAllen-Edinburg-Mission	10.9	27.1	61.9	100
MS	Jackson	13.4	15.9	70.7	100
TN-MS-AR	Memphis	13.6	14.5	71.9	100
TX	El Paso	9.2	18.6	72.2	100
LA	Baton Rouge	10.0	14.4	75.5	100
AL	Birmingham-Hoover	11.5	12.3	76.2	100
GA-SC	Augusta-Richmond County	10.5	13.2	76.3	100
LA	New Orleans-Metairie-Kenner	9.3	14.4	76.3	100
CA	Bakersfield	8.2	13.4	78.3	100
SC	Columbia	9.5	11.6	78.8	100
NC-SC	Charlotte-Gastonia-Concord	10.3	10.7	79.0	100
FL	Lakeland	9.9	10.4	79.7	100
TN-GA	Chattanooga	10.8	9.5	79.7	100
GA	Atlanta-Sandy Springs-Marietta	6.4	13.8	79.8	100
SC	Charleston-North Charleston	9.3	10.8	79.9	100
AR	Little Rock-North Little Rock	9.9	10.1	80.1	100
TX	Houston-Sugar Land-Baytown	8.2	11.7	80.1	100
NC	Greensboro-High Point	9.9	9.8	80.3	100
VA-NC	Virginia Beach-Norfolk-Newport News	6.4	13.0	80.6	100
TX	San Antonio	8.8	10.4	80.8	100
TX	Dallas-Fort Worth-Arlington	8.5	10.6	80.9	100
SC	Greenville	10.0	8.3	81.7	100
CA	Fresno	7.7	10.5	81.8	100
NV	Las Vegas-Paradise	8.2	9.8	82.0	100
FL	Jacksonville	8.0	9.6	82.4	100
CA	Riverside-San Bernardino-Ontario	6.0	11.3	82.7	100
KY-IN	Louisville-Jefferson County	7.9	9.3	82.8	100
OK	Tulsa	7.4	9.7	82.9	100
FL	Miami-Fort Lauderdale-Miami Beach	5.1	12.0	82.9	100
IN	Indianapolis-Carmel	7.9	9.2	82.9	100
FL	Orlando-Kissimmee	7.0	9.7	83.3	100
OK	Oklahoma City	6.9	9.5	83.5	100
NM	Albuquerque	5.8	10.4	83.7	100
VA	Richmond	6.6	9.6	83.8	100
AZ	Phoenix-Mesa-Scottsdale	5.5	10.5	84.0	100
NC	Raleigh-Cary	5.9	9.9	84.2	100
CA	Stockton	6.7	9.0	84.3	100
TN	Nashville-Davidson--Murfreesboro	8.2	7.3	84.5	100
OH-KY-IN	Cincinnati-Middletown	6.9	7.8	85.3	100
MI	Detroit-Warren-Livonia	5.3	9.3	85.4	100
CA	Modesto	5.7	8.8	85.5	100
KS	Wichita	6.2	8.3	85.5	100
AZ	Tucson	5.2	9.1	85.7	100
FL	Tampa-St. Petersburg-Clearwater	6.2	7.9	85.9	100

Table B.2: Percent RAL, RAC, and Non-RAL/RAC Use by Metropolitan Statistical Area, TY 2008

State(s)	Metropolitan Statistical Area	Refund Type			
		RAL	RAC	Non-RAL/RAC	Total
OH	Toledo	6.2	7.9	85.9	100
OH	Columbus	5.4	8.4	86.2	100
TN	Knoxville	7.8	6.0	86.2	100
MD	Baltimore-Towson	4.7	9.1	86.2	100
MO-IL	St. Louis	5.8	7.9	86.3	100
OH	Dayton	5.9	7.8	86.4	100
IL-IN-WI	Chicago-Naperville-Joliet	4.7	8.7	86.6	100
CO	Colorado Springs	3.4	9.8	86.8	100
CT	New Haven-Milford	4.7	8.0	87.2	100
TX	Austin-Round Rock	5.3	7.4	87.3	100
NE-IA	Omaha-Council Bluffs	4.1	8.6	87.3	100
NY	Albany-Schenectady-Troy	4.9	7.8	87.3	100
ID	Boise City-Nampa	3.8	8.9	87.3	100
MO-KS	Kansas City	5.0	7.7	87.3	100
PA-NJ-DE-MD	Philadelphia-Camden-Wilmington	4.5	8.1	87.4	100
MI	Grand Rapids-Wyoming	4.8	7.8	87.4	100
RI-MA	Providence-New Bedford-Fall River	4.7	7.8	87.5	100
OH-PA	Youngstown-Warren-Boardman	6.0	6.5	87.5	100
PA	Scranton--Wilkes-Barre	5.3	7.2	87.5	100
OH	Cleveland-Elyria-Mentor	5.0	7.4	87.6	100
UT	Salt Lake City	4.6	7.7	87.7	100
HI	Honolulu	3.9	8.3	87.8	100
NY	Syracuse	5.0	7.1	87.9	100
MI	Lansing-East Lansing	4.3	7.7	87.9	100
NY-NJ-PA	New York-Northern New Jersey-Long Island	4.1	7.9	88.0	100
OH	Akron	5.0	7.0	88.0	100
PA-NJ	Allentown-Bethlehem-Easton	4.4	7.4	88.2	100
MA	Springfield	3.8	7.9	88.2	100
FL	Palm Bay-Melbourne-Titusville	5.1	6.7	88.3	100
IA	Des Moines-West Des Moines	4.2	7.4	88.4	100
NY	Rochester	4.5	7.1	88.4	100
WI	Milwaukee-Waukesha-West Allis	4.0	7.4	88.6	100
CO	Denver-Aurora	3.7	7.7	88.7	100
PA	Harrisburg-Carlisle	4.5	6.8	88.7	100
NY	Poughkeepsie-Newburgh-Middletown	4.0	7.3	88.8	100
DC-VA-MD-WV	Washington-Arlington-Alexandria	3.1	8.0	88.9	100
CA	Los Angeles-Long Beach-Santa Ana	3.7	7.4	88.9	100
NY	Buffalo-Niagara Falls	4.6	6.3	89.0	100
FL	Sarasota-Bradenton-Venice	4.7	5.7	89.6	100
CA	Sacramento--Arden-Arcade--Roseville	3.4	6.9	89.7	100
CA	San Diego-Carlsbad-San Marcos	3.0	7.3	89.7	100
CT	Hartford-West Hartford-East Hartford	3.2	7.0	89.8	100
PA	Pittsburgh	4.1	6.0	89.9	100
PA	Lancaster	4.1	5.8	90.2	100

Table B.2: Percent RAL, RAC, and Non-RAL/RAC Use by Metropolitan Statistical Area, TY 2008

State(s)	Metropolitan Statistical Area	Refund Type			
		RAL	RAC	Non-RAL/RAC	Total
MA	Worcester	2.9	6.8	90.3	100
CA	Oxnard-Thousand Oaks-Ventura	3.2	6.4	90.4	100
ME	Portland-South Portland-Biddeford	2.8	6.7	90.5	100
WA	Seattle-Tacoma-Bellevue	3.8	5.6	90.7	100
OR-WA	Portland-Vancouver-Beaverton	2.5	6.4	91.1	100
CT	Bridgeport-Stamford-Norwalk	2.9	5.0	92.1	100
MA-NH	Boston-Cambridge-Quincy	2.3	5.6	92.2	100
MN-WI	Minneapolis-St. Paul-Bloomington	1.9	5.2	92.9	100
WI	Madison	1.9	5.1	93.0	100
CA	Santa Rosa-Petaluma	1.9	5.0	93.1	100
CA	San Francisco-Oakland-Fremont	2.0	4.5	93.5	100
CA	San Jose-Sunnyvale-Santa Clara	1.9	4.0	94.0	100
	Total	6.2	8.6	85.3	100

Source: Authors' calculations of IRS taxpayer data.
Universe: All tax filers with a return.

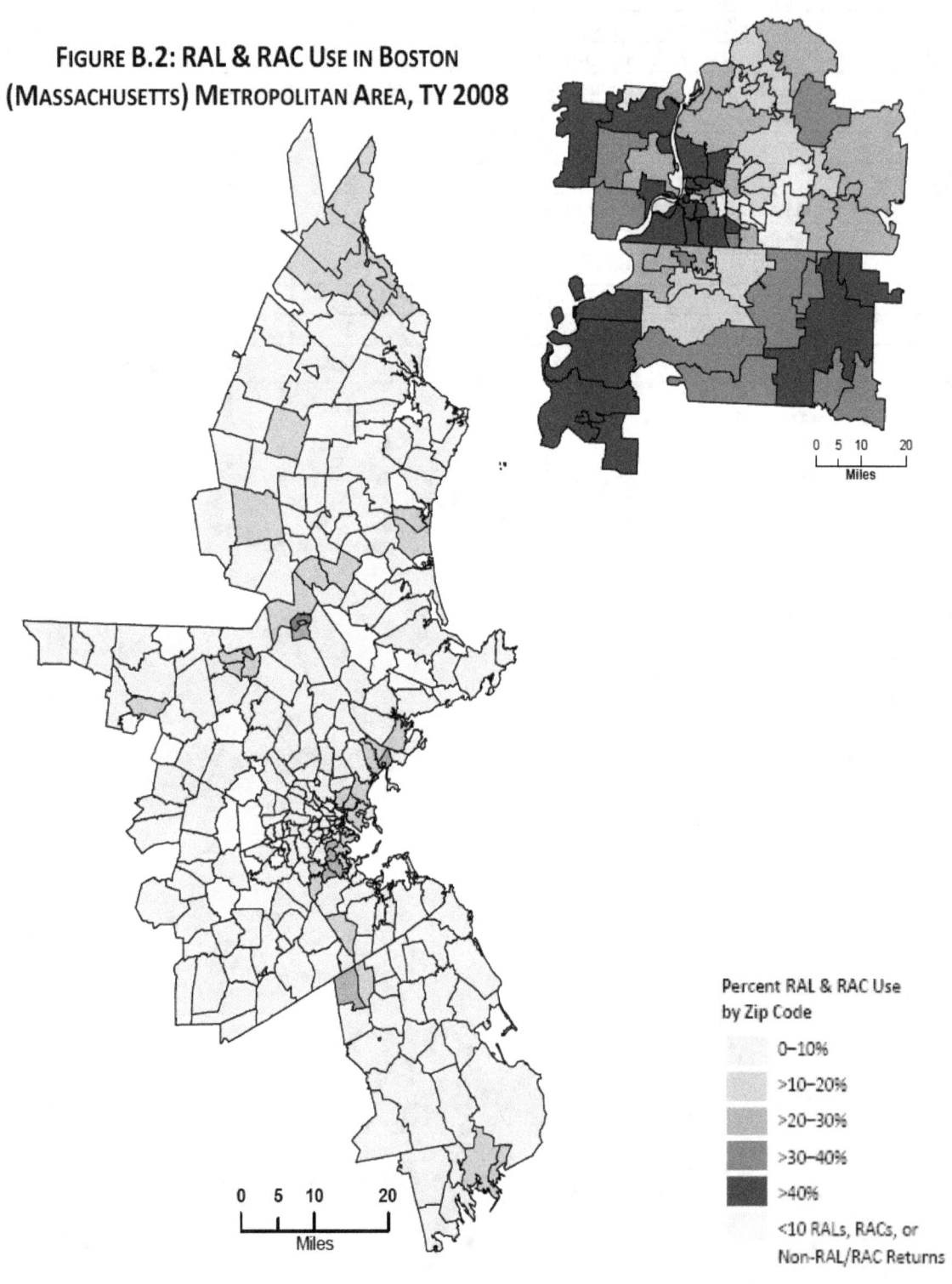

FIGURE B.1: RAL & RAC USE IN MEMPHIS (TENNESSEE) METROPOLITAN AREA, TY 2008

FIGURE B.2: RAL & RAC USE IN BOSTON (MASSACHUSETTS) METROPOLITAN AREA, TY 2008

Percent RAL & RAC Use by Zip Code

0–10%
>10–20%
>20–30%
>30–40%
>40%
<10 RALs, RACs, or Non-RAL/RAC Returns

Source: Authors' calculations of IRS taxpayer data.
Universe: All tax filers with a return and living in zip codes with >10 RAL, RAC, or Non-RAL/RAC total returns; approximately 98 percent of tax filers with a return.

FIGURE B.3: RAL & RAC USE IN JACKSONVILLE (FLORIDA) METROPOLITAN AREA, TY 2008

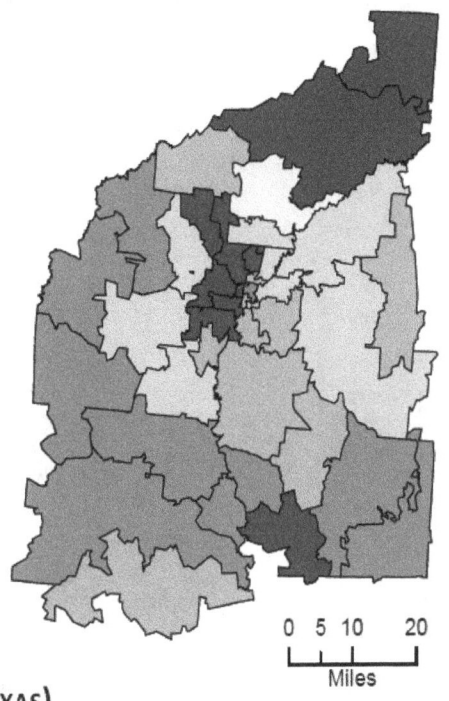

FIGURE B.4: RAL & RAC USE IN EL PASO (TEXAS) METROPOLITAN AREA, TY 2008

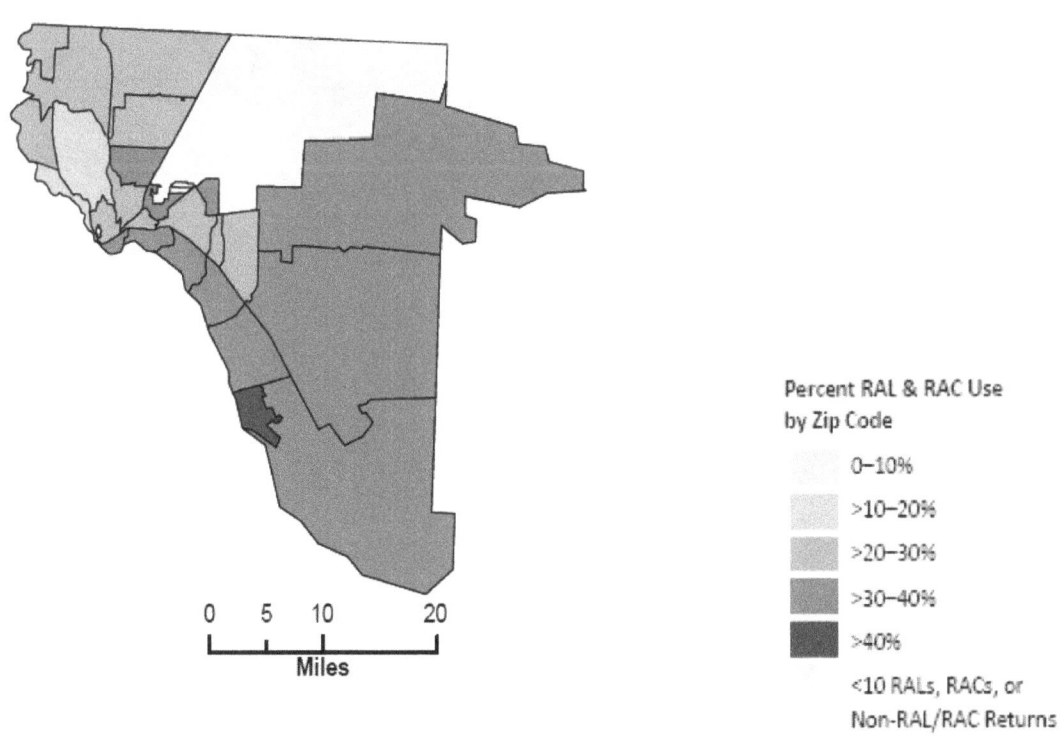

Percent RAL & RAC Use by Zip Code

- 0–10%
- >10–20%
- >20–30%
- >30–40%
- >40%
- <10 RALs, RACs, or Non-RAL/RAC Returns

Source: Authors' calculations of IRS taxpayer data.
Universe: All tax filers with a return and living in zip codes with >10 RAL, RAC, or Non-RAL/RAC total returns; approximately 98 percent of tax filers with a return.

FIGURE B. 5: RAL & RAC USE IN ST. LOUIS (MISSOURI) METROPOLITAN AREA, TY 2008

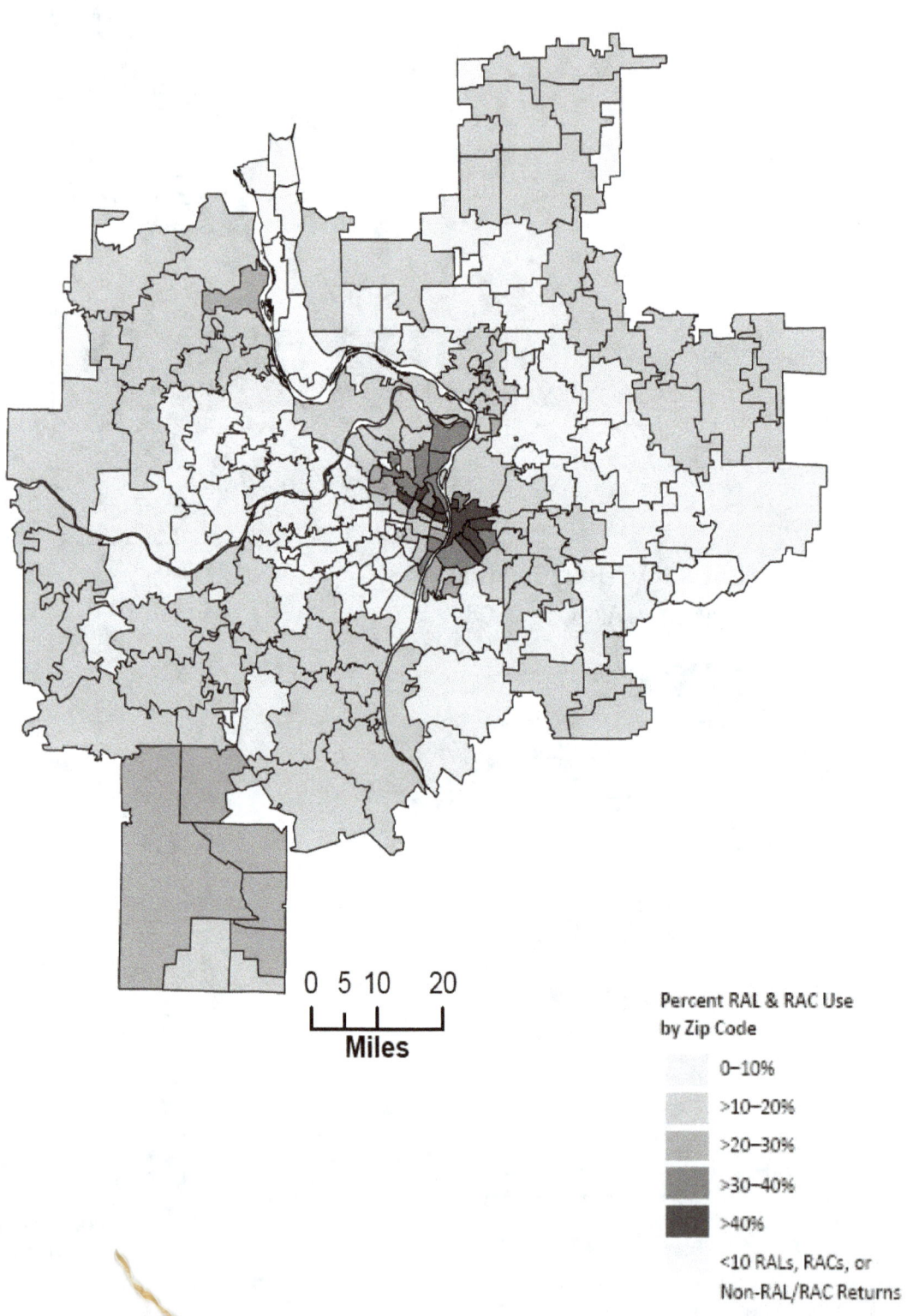

Source: Authors' calculations of IRS taxpayer data.
Universe: All tax filers with a return and living in zip codes with >10 RAL, RAC, or Non-RAL/RAC total returns; approximately 98 percent of tax filers with a return.

www.ingramcontent.com/pod-product-compliance
Lightning Source LLC
Chambersburg PA
CBHW081903170526
45167CB00007B/3132